The road to town before Newport got an industrial estate and traffic lights.

LAUNCESTON

Some Pages in History

FRONT COVER

The Round House, Newport, Launceston, from an old engraving - probably early 19th century. It has the shaft of an ancient cross at the centre, and was where Members of Parliament for Newport were elected in the 18th century. The erection of railings at the entrance by the town council recently caused a chorus of protests, but this picture shows there is nothing new in railings.

BACK COVER

St. Thomas Hill (Old Hill) was a popular subject for artists, and H. B. Wimbush painted a picture of it for a set of Oilette postcards produced by Raphael Tuck. In the distance is St. Stephens Church.

JOAN RENDELL

LAUNCESTON

Some Pages in History

Landfall Publications
1993

First published 1993 by
LANDFALL PUBLICATIONS
Landfall, Penpol, Devoran, Truro, Cornwall TR3 6NW
Telephone: 0872-862581

Copyright © Joan Rendell 1993

A CIP catalogue record for this book is available from the British Library.

ISBN 1 873443 12 9

All rights reserved. No part of this book may be reproduced or transmitted in any form or by any means including recording or photocopying, without permission in writing from the publisher.

Printed by the Troutbeck Press
and bound by R. Booth Ltd., Antron Hill, Mabe, Penryn, Cornwall

CONTENTS

JOAN RENDELL 8

ACKNOWLEDGEMENTS 9

INTRODUCTION 11

CHAPTER 1 Launceston as a Market Town 13

CHAPTER 2 The Church Scene 23

CHAPTER 3 Money, Money, Money! 34

CHAPTER 4 Launceston's Turnpike Trust 37

CHAPTER 5 Rip Roaring Launceston! 43

CHAPTER 6 Gaols and Punishment 48

CHAPTER 7 Launceston as a Parole Town 53

CHAPTER 8 The Second Military Invasion 61

CHAPTER 9 Trade and Industry 66

CHAPTER 10 Launceston Miscellany 75

BYGONE LAUNCESTON A selection of photographs of scenes
                        not specifically referred to in the text
   Days of Steam 78
   Transport 80
   "Lanson" Looked Like This 82
   When People Get Together 89

CONCLUSION 94

LANDFALL PUBLICATIONS 95

Joan Rendell photographed recently in her Bardic robes by Stephen d'Entrecasteaux.
(In her own words: "My own mug, wrinkles and all. Why didn't I discover Oil of Ulay in my youth?")

JOAN RENDELL

The author was born in Launceston, where her family on her mother's side go back to the early 18th century. Her mother was born in Helston and her father was a member of an old St. Austell family, so her roots are deep in Cornwall.

Trained as an artist, she switched to writing in the 1960s and this will be her 21st published book. She has covered such diverse subjects as matchbox labels (of which she has one of the largest collections in the world and is recognised as an international authority), crafts, flower arranging, natural history and local history. Several of her books have been published also in the U.S.A., Australia and Japan. She is a regular contributor to a number of national and international magazines, with articles on a wide range of subjects.

She is a Bard of the Cornish Gorseth with the Bardic name of Scryfer Weryn (Writer of Werrington - her home parish), and has for many years been closely involved with voluntary work, honoured by being made a Member of the Order of the British Empire and the holder of the Queen's Silver Jubilee Medal for service to the community. She is an honorary life member of several national and local organisations, including the British Matchbox Label & Booklet Society, The Japan Society of London, The Friends of Lawrence House Museum and the Launceston Floral Art Group, and she has been Clerk to Werrington Parish Council for nearly 50 years, starting as one of the youngest Clerks in the country. She is a past President of the Federation of Old Cornwall Societies, and its present Honorary Secretary.

Joan Rendell also fulfils a busy lecturing programme and has made many TV and radio broadcasts. She also contributes to several newspapers as a freelance journalist.

ACKNOWLEDGEMENTS

The author is indebted to the following for all their help, for permission to examine documents, for information, for access to privately held archives and for loan of photographs:

Cornwall County Record Office; Devon County Record Office; Cornish Studies Library; Westcountry Studies Library, Exeter; Cornwall Archaeological Unit; British Numismatic Society; Cornish & Devon Post; English Heritage; Trustees and curators, Lawrence House Museum; Mr K. Battin; Mr G. Bishop; Mrs M. Chapman; Mr John Ellacott; Mr R. Gilbert; Miss J. Jones; late Mr W. Maunder; Mr and Mrs C. Moss; Mrs B. Penno; Miss L. Pearce; late Mrs Mabel Petherick; Mrs L. C. Pooley; Mr K. Rowe; Mrs Roy Sloman; Mrs P. Smart; late Canon W. Steer; Mr and Mrs L. Stonelake; Mr Mike Stoneman; Mr Henry Symons; Mr and Mrs Russell Symons; Mr A. B. Venning (for loan of an unpublished ms.); Mr and Mrs Philip Warren; Mr and Mrs Robert Williams (for access to privately held archives).

Everywhere co-operation, interest and encouragement have been given in abundance, from both individuals and the staffs of the offices and libraries which have been visited. Thank you to everyone.

Pooley's shop, Westgate Street, was formerly the Dolphin Inn. It later became Raddall's and was burnt down about 1968. This drawing was done in 1937.

INTRODUCTION

This book is *not* a comprehensive history of Launceston; it is, for want of a better description, filling in some of the gaps.

Such features as St. Stephens and St. Thomas Churches, the Priory, John Wesley's connection with Launceston, education in Launceston, the history of the Feudal Dues, political aspects, etc., etc., have all been dealt with in publications by other authors in the past. The object of this book is to probe into subjects which have not before received much in-depth attention and to use as much previously unpublished material as possible in both text and photographs.

There are probably more subjects which have been left unexplored but publishers set authors a deadline and are not prepared to wait indefinitely - which is as long as it would take to record *every*thing that has happened in Launceston over the years. Also a book has to sell at a realistic price and not be so thick and heavy that lifting it from the bookcase is a task to be avoided!

So, if your special interest is not included it is probably being looked into and will doubtless find its way into print some time in the future. Only so much can be crammed into a lifetime!

Joan Rendell,
Werrington,
Launceston.

1993

The line of the old drovers' road, now running through a field, almost parallel with the present B3254 road, from what is now the Egloskerry road junction to Rockwell, Yeolmbridge.

CHAPTER 1
Launceston as a Market Town

From time immemorial Launceston has been known as a market town; as far back as the 10th century Saxon St. Stephens was reputed to have an important market, which could be the reason that several of the ancient drovers' tracks converged there.

There is a fairly clear time fix for the ending of the market at St. Stephens, contained in no less an authority than the Domesday Book, because in folio 120b the following entry may be seen:-
"The Canons of St. Stephen held Lanscavetone. There are four hides of land which were never subject to the payment of geld. There is land for twenty ploughs. There are three ploughs and three leagues of pasture, and sixty acres of wood. It was formerly worth eight pounds. Now it is worth four pounds.

From this manor the Count of Mortain took away a market which lay there in the time of King Edward (the Confessor) and was worth twenty shillings."

Robert, Count of Mortain did, of course, build the walled town or burgh of Dunhevet around his castle of Dunhevet and it was to there that he transferred the market which up to King Edward's time was the original town of the Canons of St. Stephen's, then known as Lanstefanton.

In their "Histories of Launceston and Dunheved" published in 1885 Messrs R. and O. B. Peter quote from a charter of Reginald de Dunstanville, Earl of Cornwall, 1140-1176, a natural son of Henry I. This includes the passage "... when the Count of Mortain transferred the Sunday market from the town of St. Stephen at Lanstone, to the new town of the Castle of Dunhevet, the Canons of Lanstone, with the assent and will of the aforesaid Count of Mortain, retained for themselves and their borough of Landstone, and the Burgesses remaining in it, all liberties pertaining to a free borough ... except only the Sunday market."

Sadly in recent years the market in Launceston has declined and now there are even doubts cast by some on whether Launceston can still be classed as a market town. In the 1990s controversy raged over whether or not a purpose built cattle market should be provided on the outskirts of the town or in neighbouring parishes but only time will tell whether or not Launceston regains its former importance as a market town.

In the past Launceston had a fine reputation for its market - both cattle and produce. Traces of the old drovers' tracks dating from medieval times and even before that, still exist; some are today's roads, their line unchanged over centuries.

For instance, Pig or Piggy Lane which leads off the Launceston - Egloskerry road and is signposted 'Yeolmbridge', passing the great barrow of Race Hill Down, was a branch of the once important track which from Barricadoes Gate led to North Petherwin along a ridge of barrows. The Piggy Lane road twists and leads down a steep hill to the present day B3254 road on Barricadoes hill but the line of the old road is still clearly visible, crossing the main road and running along through a field to Yeolmbridge, its boundaries marked by a line of age old trees which border it, emerging at Rockwell to join the present road over Yeolmbridge bridge. Originally it crossed the River Attery at a natural ford just above the bridge at Yeolmbridge and was what is now the lane beside the Clubroom, straight on until it met the present road just above Ducky Pools.

Right up until 1929-30 cattle being brought to Launceston market from North Petherwin, Egloskerry and even beyond that were rested in accommodation fields behind the houses in St. Stephens Hill, where they were kept to regain weight after their long walk, before being offered for sale in the market. Anyone who owned any of these fields was entitled to an extra Parliamentary vote. The onset of 'foot and mouth' disease ended the practice because animals were no longer allowed on the land. By the time it was deemed safe to revive it, motorised transport of animals had commenced and Glover & Uglow's cattle lorries were a familiar sight around the district, although some farmers still continued to walk cattle to market or the railway station right up to the time of the closure of the railway in the town.

Some of the early tracks were, of course, more important than others, depending on the amount of traffic which used them. Robbins, in his 19th century "History of Launceston", refers to the Royal Duchy Road which was something equivalent to a motorway of its day, running the length of Cornwall. A small section of this ancient track still exists as a narrow green lane running for a few hundred yards close to the present day Launceston by-pass.

But to get back to Launceston as a market town. Prior to 1840 everything was sold in the streets, from cattle to provisions, from rope to skins to sweetmeats. Shopkeepers boarded up their windows on cattle market day and among the melee of cattle, sheep, farmers and drovers, stallholders set up their 'stannins'. There is an old west Cornwall saying which the writer's mother often quoted when illustrating doggedness or advice not to 'give way' on any issue - "stick to your stannin' if you only sell a ha'porth".

Over the years the market had spread out to encompass most of the Launceston town centre and in 1839 the Mayor, Aldermen and Burgesses of the Borough decided it was time to call a halt to this and announced that by the holding of the market the streets and other thoroughfares "are obstructed and rendered dangerous and inconvenient to the Inhabitants of the Town and the Public at large" and they further decided to provide "a proper Market Place or Places and Buildings, with all other Conveniences necessary there unto and suitable approaches to the same".

Before this could take place an Act of Parliament had to be sought and granted and in June 1840 such an Act was obtained.

A popular architect of the day, George Wightwick, was commissioned to design the market buildings and came up with a suggestion for two separate buildings - an Upper and a Lower Market. Wightwick, a Welshman, had set up practice in Plymouth; he was not highly regarded as an architect because he was not considered sufficiently imaginative but he was quite popular for designing market buildings and among a number of commissions in Cornwall he designed the Chapel of St. Michael and All Angels (later to become the parish church) at Bude and the market building at Callington, so he was obviously deemed suitable for Launceston work. In recent years doubt has been cast on the assumption that the buildings actually erected *were* to the designs submitted by Wightwick but there appears to be no proof either way.

The ambitious plan for two buildings meant considerable sacrifice for some of the town's residents and landowners. The Mayor and Council gave themselves the power "to purchase and take so much of the several Messuages, Houses, Buildings, Land, Tenements and Hereditaments as the said Council may think necessary and proper to be taken" and no less than sixty six properties were listed as being possible subjects for demolition. They included The East Cornwall Bank in Broad Street, The Turk's Head public house in Church Street, the London Inn in Church Street, an unnamed bank in Broad Street, a melting house in Blindhole where occupier John Doidge melted down animal fat for the making of tallow candles, workshops, butchers' shambles and cellars, stables, shops, and the engine house in Church Street, owned by the Mayor, Aldermen and Burgesses and used to garage the fire engine, all of which illustrates how very congested Launceston town centre must have been at that time.

The demolition area included offices in Butter Market and Back Street, which was the area on the north and south sides of what is now The Square and in which dairy produce was sold. The well-to-do and the humble were equally affected in the great clear-out. Richard Dingley's bank was on the list, as were the Duke of Northumberland's stable, gig house and courtlage (sic) in Church Style and a dwelling house, stable and garden owned by His Grace and occupied by the Reverend George Buckmaster Gibbons. The Turnpike Trustees' stable in Blindhole was to go, along with Mary Mann's tiny cottage in Southgate Street and Anne Cudlipp's plantation, stable, garden and outhouses in Blindhole, with much else besides. All in all it looked like being a clean sweep, but did contain clauses providing for compensation.

Incidentally, looking at Blindhole today one wonders how on earth all the buildings, gardens and even a plantation were squeezed into it. Anne Cudlipp, quite a considerable landowner at that time, had in addition to her own plantation, stable and outhouses, a garden occupied by William

LAUNCESTON AS A MARKET TOWN

The Upper Market House, better known as the Butter Market, in its heyday.

Launceston Pannier Market in Race Hill, 1993.

LAUNCESTON AS A MARKET TOWN

Westgate Street and the Butter Market.

Back Lane, with the Butter Market on the left.

The Town beam and scales and measures, now in Lawrence House Museum.

Close-up of the Town bushel measure.

Dymond, a house and stable occupied by John Palmer, a stable and gig house occupied by Dr John Travers Lawrence, a stable, cellars and the melting house occupied by John Doidge (who actually lived in a dwelling house, also owned by Anne Cudlipp, in Church Street); also in Blindhole were the dwelling house, stable and garden occupied by Rev'd Gibbons, a barn and stable owned and occupied by William Smith, a dwelling house and courtlage owned by Mrs Kittow and occupied by Thomas Anstis Braddon, The Launceston Turnpike Trustees' stable occupied by "their Survey", John Huxham, who also occupied a dwelling house, stable, lofts, cellars and buildings in Blindhole. And those stables are still there today, now used as a store but still with cobbled floor and old beams.

Probably the thing of greatest interest today is the variety of goods sold in the markets and the toll charges - both seem somewhat amusing in these vastly different times. Charges included:-
Every bull, ox, cow or heifer exposed for sale 3d. Cow and calf 3d. Head of swine 2d. Horse, gelding, mare, colt, filly, mule or ass 6d. Carcase of hog or pork pig 1d. Pannier of sucking pigs 2d. Cart with sucking pigs exposed for sale 6d. Tallow of bullocks, sheep and lambs 1d. Score of sheep or sheep and lambs 2/-. Pannier or basket of fish 4d. Bullock's hide 1d. Calf's hide ½d. Sheep and lamb's skin ¼d. Pack or pad of wool 1/-. Cart of potatoes or turnips 8d. Wheelbarrow ditto 2d. Bag ditto 1d. Handbasket, hamper or other things of poultry, butter or eggs 2d. Ditto of fruit and vegetables 1d. Apple trees, shrubs and plants 1d a foot. Waggonload of hay, straw or corn in the straw 6d. Cartload ditto 3d. Imperial bushel of wheat, barley or oats 2d. Every 56lbs of flour or clover seeds 1/-. Ditto trefoil, turnip or eaver seeds 6d. 100 cabbage plants ½d.

All articles were weighed at the beam and scales kept in the market, at a charge of 2d per cwt. or ½d for every 28lbs, and were measured by the measures kept in the market, at ½d per bushel or any less quantity. This was strictly enforced and every effort made to ensure that nobody cheated. It was the forerunner of today's Trading Standards. There was also a slaughterhouse run in conjunction with the market, where slaughtering charges ranged from 1/- to 2d per animal.

Great Market Days were then held on the first Thursday in March and the third Thursday in April every year and tolls were increased on those days. Ordinary market days were Wednesday and Saturday.

Now Great Market Days are no longer held. As everyone knows, the main market day is now Tuesday and the pannier market in a modern building in Race Hill is also open on Saturdays. Thursday, once a Great Market Day, is, of course, now early closing day in the town.

The Upper or Butter Market was demolished after World War I to make way for the war memorial, a dignified structure which is an asset to the town centre. It was only in its latter years of existence that the Upper Market was known as the Butter Market. The clock which was a prominent feature of it was originally on the Assize Hall, which in its turn was demolished to make way for the Upper Market, and now the clock is above the main entrance to the Town Hall, along with the 17th century hammer jacks which accompanied it.

The quarter jacks, known locally as the Black Jacks

The clock itself is reputed to have come from Hexworthy, former home of Col. Bennett, an ardent supporter of Oliver Cromwell, who is said to have stayed at Hexworthy on at least one occasion.

The Lower Market ceased being used as the pannier market over twenty years ago although the fish market in the cellars below remained from some time afterwards and one fish shop was still housed there up to the 1990s. The steps which led down to the fish market disappeared when the Market House became a shopping arcade. After a spell as a furniture showroom the Lower Market Building was turned into an arcade housing a number of shops and an ornamental fountain was installed in the centre of the floor space. It is still an imposing building with its clerestory design; it was built to last and it has done so; George Wightwick could at least be proud of that.

As a footnote it should be noted that the Town Council of the time was not to lose any opportunity of emphasising its rights to all and everything pertaining to its new market: it even had written into its 1840 Launceston market Act "all the Dirt, Dust, Dung, Ashes, and Filth to be swept, gathered and collected in or from the said Market Place or Places ... shall belong to and be the Property of ... and absolutely vested in the said Council for the purposes of this Act". Hardly valuable property, one would think!

Flowers piled around the war memorial after its unveiling in 1921

The unveiling of the war memorial on the site of the Butter Market. The ceremony was performed by the Lord Lieutenant of Cornwall on Sunday 30th October 1921. The foundation stone had been laid by Edward, Prince of Wales on 25th May 1921.

The procession to St. Mary Magdalene Church after the unveiling of the war memorial.

The Square and war memorial in the 1950s.

The Butter Market being demolished in 1919.

The Lower Market House as it is today.

Guildhall Square and the Hender family memorial with drinking troughs for horses and dogs, prior to its removal for road improvements in the 1980s.

CHAPTER 2
The Church Scene

Much has been written about Launceston's churches. Historians down the ages have been fascinated, especially by the magnificence of St. Mary Magdalene, the town's parish church. Claimed quite rightly, to be unique in the British Isles in the matter of its extraordinary carved granite exterior, it incorporates so many interesting features that almost half a day can be spent examining and investigating all of them.

Take a look at the most dominant feature - the tower. In days of yore they built to last; that tower has been there for over six hundred years, as solid today as when it was constructed. The tower was built at the instigation of Edward, the Black Prince, Duke of Cornwall, presumably to enhance the chantry chapel which stood alongside and which was subsequently extended and was in 1380 licensed to serve the residents of the town of Launceston.

Prior to this, a chapel within the castle precincts was the townspeople's main place of worship but after the demise of the Black Prince the castle and its surroundings were left to deteriorate and when the chapel of St. Mary Magdalene was improved and enlarged the castle chapel fell into disrepair and eventual oblivion.

It is believed that the original tower nearly had another built beside it. Although there is no documentary evidence to support this, examination of the present church and its relation to the tower suggests an intention to construct another tower.

The story of the building of the church is well known. In the year 1511 Sir Henry Trecarrell had grandiose plans for rebuilding his home, Trecarrell Manor in the parish of Lezant, and this was to incorporate a chapel dedicated to St. Mary Magdalene. He engaged the finest stonemasons to carve the decoration on the hard granite and all was proceeding according to plan when, so the legend tells us, Sir Henry's infant son and heir was tragically drowned whilst being bathed by a nursemaid, who, neglecting the child for just a moment to attend to another duty, returned to find he had fallen face down in the water and had drowned. The shock is said to have killed the baby's mother, who died a week later.

These devastating occurrences so demoralised Sir Henry that he abandoned his plans for a new house and instead decided to use all his building materials to create a new church in Launceston. The work was completed and the church dedicated on 18th June 1524.

Between the end of the church and the existing tower a large gap was left. It has always been assumed that this was to have accommodated a tower. Did Sir Henry intend to demolish the Black Prince's tower and build one to match his new church? We shall never know. Various theories have been put forward as to why this end of the church was never actually completed but it can only be conjecture: as far as is known Sir Henry never left any written evidence of his intentions.

With a gap between the end of the church and its tower it was inevitable that in a town tightly packed within its town walls such a space would be utilised and first two cottages were built in it. These were subsequently demolished in the early 19th century when the then Duke of Northumberland, as Constable of the Castle and owner of Werrington Park and extensive property in the town, had the cottages cleared away and in their place erected a Council Room, a sort of minor Town Hall, for the use of the Corporation of the town. When the Guildhall was built in 1881 it became redundant and is now the choir vestry, a useful adjunct to the church. The position of the gable end of the cottages is still clearly visible on the side of the tower beneath the clock.

THE CHURCH SCENE

The tower did not always contain a clock but it did have the distinction of housing the first public clock in Cornwall, put there in 1431, a one handed affair.

Years ago, when children were not as sophisticated as they are now, they had the pleasure and interest of a myriad of fairy tales told to them by adults and one of these concerned the clock in St. Mary's Church tower. We were always told that the hole in the tower which contained the clock was big enough for a carriage and pair to be driven through it. From ground level it seemed improbable but the grown-ups said it was so and thus it had to be believed. Then in the 1980s the woodwork surrounding the clock had become rotten and after a piece broke off and fell into the street it was deemed highly dangerous and the whole clock was removed for repair and refurbishment, leaving temporarily a gaping hole in the tower. When the clock was lowered to the ground it attracted quite a lot of attention and it was then that the old fairy story was shown to be more or less true. The clock when seen at ground level is so huge that the hole from which it came could certainly accommodate some sort of equipage. It would probably be big enough for a pony and trap to be driven through - even if the carriage and pair was a bit of an exaggeration it proved that we should always have faith in what our parents tell us!

It would be of considerable interest to know just who designed the elaborate decoration of the exterior of Sir Henry's church. He appears to have been extremely keen on symbolism so it is quite likely that he designed all the decoration himself or at least instructed someone in what he wanted.

Around the porch are reputed to be carved representations of all the plants mentioned in the Bible as being used in the preparation of the ointment with which Mary anointed Christ's feet as He hung on the Cross. Weathering over the centuries has resulted in making identification extremely difficult but past generations have recorded that they are all depicted.

Above the porch is carved a shield bearing the arms of Sir Henry Trecarrell quartered with those of his wife, Margaret Kelway. The correct description of the shield bearing these arms is two chevrons sable and argent two bones in saltire sable between two pears.

Also above the porch are carved representations of St. George slaying the dragon and St. Martin sharing his cloak with the beggar. On each side of the doorway is carved an ostrich plume, part of the arms of the Duchy of Cornwall - The Prince of Wales's Feathers as they were once popularly

The late Canon W. Steer and the late Canon M. Andrews outside the main door of St. Mary Magdalene Church on the occasion of the first flower festival held there.

known.

High above the porch is a little niche which obviously was intended to hold a statuette, presumably St. Mary Magdalene. What happened to the original is not known, but it was probably removed prior to the Reformation. In 1915 a terracotta statuette of St. Mary Magdalene was placed there by the Ching family as a memorial to Capt. Lawrence Ching, R.N., who died in 1911.

Whether out of vanity or on the advice of his architect, Sir Henry Trecarrell had portraits of himself and his wife carved into the stone and incorporated quite prominently into the facade of the church, although today the casual visitor often fails to notice them. Doubtless 16th century worshippers and visitors were more observant. The faces are part of the decoration around the first window right beside the porch and it must be said that they are hardly flattering. Sir Henry looks slightly alarmed and his lady does not look very well pleased at being sculpted in stone but it must have been quite an undertaking to carve any features at all in the hard granite.

TIME STANDS STILL

TIME is standing still for St. Mary's Church, Launceston for its clock face has just been removed for renovation.

Last September a £5,000 appeal was launched to pay for repair and renovation works but so far only enough money has been received to take the face down.

"The problem is people do not see the repairs as an emergency. It would be different if it was the roof that needed the repair said Rev. Robert Watton, vicar of St. Mary's.

Mr. Watton explained the clock face had to be removed for safety reasons as wooden frames and surrounds had rotten away and the clock face was in danger of falling to the ground.

The clock will now be repaired, regilded and overhauled and if sufficient funds are raised it is hoped to put the two clock faces back before the winter.

One of the faces mesures about 1oft in width with its numerals standing about 1ft. high and was removed by steeplejacks on Wednesday evening.

Renovation of the faces needs careful attention and is done about every fifty years. Mr. Watton explained that although the present clck faces date from 1824 the site where the face hangs is the site of the first public clock in Cornwall which is believed to have been hung in 1433.

Already Launceston Town Council and other bodies have given money towards the renovation work but the vicar is hoping more support will be received from local businesses.

When the clock underwent repairs in 1888 by a Birmingham firm the work which included a new hand, painting and renovation work cost £58.17s 6d.

The face of time which will soon be renovated, with Rev. Robert Watton looking on. Pictures: Ron Cable.

Article and photographs courtesy "Cornish & Devon Post".

THE CHURCH SCENE

Sir Henry and Lady Trecarrell portrayed in stone on St. Mary Magdalene Church.

The reversed "E" stone on St. Mary Magdalene Church, with the "correct" E beside it.

The Arms of King Henry VIII carved above the window of St. Mary Magdalene Church.

THE CHURCH SCENE

For those who have the interest and patience to examine closely the complete pattern of the exterior of the church there can be traced a series of shields above the plinth encircling the building. The first ones appear to be blank, although they are so badly weathered that that may not have been the original case, and some carry the Trecarrell Arms, but from the chancel door onwards each alternate shield is carved with a letter or a kind of punctuation mark and at first glance they seem to be meaningless. However, that is not so. They spell out, in Latin, the following phrases: "Hail, Mary full of grace; the Lord be with thee; the bridegroom loves the bride. Mary chose the best part. O, how terrible and fearful is this place; truly this is no other than the House of God and the Gate of Heaven". A strange series of phrases, but there is one even greater curiosity in this chain of shields: at the north east corner is one which appears to have the number '3' on it and one is left wondering how it fits into the text. But it is not a '3' at all, it is the letter 'E' placed the wrong way round. In the past chroniclers have suggested that the mason who set the stone way back in the 16th century was probably illiterate and when he came to place the 'E' stone he inserted it upside down and backwards. Not at all. He was either very cunning or had received instructions to place the stone in just such a position. In Civil War days a carved letter 'E' placed 'back to front' on a building was part of a code which indicated that the owner or occupier had Royalist sympathies. Examples may be also seen at Penfound manor, near Bude and at Werrington Park, among other buildings.

Sir Henry was obviously a Royalist sympathiser as he had the arms of King Henry VIII carved above the fine east window on the exterior of his church (another form of insurance against losing his head if the King was displeased with him!) and so the Royalist code symbol was probably included on his instructions.

Beneath the East window is quite the best-known piece of sculpture on the exterior of the church - the recumbent figure of St. Mary Magdalene with beside her the pot of spikenard ointment. This was obviously never intended to be treated in a light hearted way but over the years legend and tradition built up around it and from long beyond living memory it was regarded as a provider of good luck - if one possessed a certain skill. The skill consisted of being able to toss a small stone so that it landed and remained on the back of the recumbent figure. If this could be achieved the thrower was assured of good luck and in olden times this luck was believed to consist of a suit of clothes. In later years it was construed as a financial windfall or just general good fortune. In later and more affluent times, too, a small coin took the place of a stone and many were the farthings and ha'pennies, even pennies, tossed up on Mary's back and allowed to remain there, untouched. In more recent years the old custom of a stone instead of a coin has returned - money, even of the most humble denominations, is never left alone for very long these days and a pile of it just sitting there waiting for the taking would be far too great a temptation.

In the 16th and 17th centuries St. Mary's Church was famed for its minstrels. In those days large churches had minstrels, not choirs as today, and St. Mary's musicians were apparently famed far and wide. They are all depicted on the carving surrounding the figure of St. Mary Magdalene, grasping or playing their respective instruments, including the Cornish bagpipes. Some of the carvings have, sadly, weathered very badly and are now hardly recognisable.

However, careful inspection reveals that they are the rebeck, a three-stringed fiddle; the shwan, an ancient wind instrument similar to a clarinet; the clarion, a kind of trumpet with a narrow tube and a loud and clear note; the Cornish bagpipe, an instrument of great antiquity which consists of a small leather bag and pipes, very different from the better known Scottish variety; the lute, a stringed instrument somewhat resembling a guitar; the harp and a kind of hand organ to which we are unable to put a name. Note the conductor, carrying a baton and wearing a heavy chain of office around his neck.

Possibly the most poignant carving on the exterior of the church is the one least often seen by the general public. It is above the north door and it depicts a candle, the light of which is being extinguished by a snuffer. It is believed to represent the extinguishing of the young life in whose memory the magnificent church was built: Sir Henry's last tribute to the heir who never succeeded him. However much Sir Henry may or may not have been involved in the overall design of his church this small feature was almost surely his and his alone.

The interior of St. Mary's Church is just as interesting as the exterior but in a very different sort of way. For one thing there are no reminders of Sir Henry Trecarrell - he is commemorated on the outside, inside it is the turn of others.

The church has some unusual monuments, perhaps the most curious of which is the Piper cenotaph, about which more later. The Piper family

THE CHURCH SCENE

The figure of St. Mary Magdalene on the exterior of St. Mary's Church.

The St. Mary's Minstrels.

made their mark on Launceston and its environs at the same time as Sir Henry built his church but unlike him they have left no great and noble monument like St. Mary's Church, although they did enhance its interior.

Families come and families go. Some dominate for perhaps several centuries and then, for seemingly no reason at all, lapse into obscurity except for the exploits of their forebears. Such was the case with the Pipers. The family sprang into fame in the 16th century and exerted considerable influence for two hundred years after William Piper settled in Launceston (from we know not where) just before the dissolution of the Priory. He seemed to rise in the town hierarchy pretty quickly - was it money or his powers of leadership that singled him out? That we shall never know. However, he became Mayor in 1534 and the following year was granted a 'plum' sixty year lease of the Town Mill where, by ancient custom, all the townsfolk were bound to take their corn to be ground. Some people at that time might have thought it was a bit of inside dealing; the lust for power was as great in those days as it is today but these sorts of events were not documented then in the way that they are today.

William having thus distinguished himself, he was succeeded by his son Sampson who became an even brighter star in the Launceston firmament, being Mayor four times between 1566 and 1587 and furthermore, being one of eight Aldermen named in Queen Elizabeth I's Grant of Arms to Dunheved in 1573. Quite a successful lad it would seem. He died in 1592 and the family tradition was carried on by his son Arthur, who rose to even *more* dizzy heights by being made Mayor no fewer than six times between 1606 and 1644.

But all this was parochial. By far the best-known member of the family was Arthur's son Hugh, later Sir Hugh Piper, born in 1611, who went down in history for his exploits in the Civil War when he joined the famous Sir Bevil Grenville of Stowe in the Royalist cause. His first engagement was near to home, on Launceston's Windmill Hill, where he and his men repulsed strong Parliamentarian forces led by James Chudleigh, a general whose name is perpetuated by his descendants still resident in the area. Until very recent times the line of the redoubt at Windmill Hill could still be traced and several cannon balls have been excavated from the site from time to time. Unfortunately, all traces disappeared when houses were built on the site in the 1980s.

Sir Hugh also played a prominent part in the Battle of Stratton, then the siege of Plymouth and finally moved on to the great battle of Lansdown, near Bath, where he was severely wounded. They were brave men those Civil War generals: they fought and fell alongside their men; for them there was no sheltering in command posts far behind the enemy lines; they were 'up front' all the time. "A great soldier and a great gentleman" were words spoken of Sir Hugh Piper at the time.

The marble tablet from the memorial to Sir Hugh Piper in St. Mary Magdalene Church.

THE CHURCH SCENE

Sir Hugh acquired vast acreages of land and many properties around Launceston. Prior to the Restoration he and his wife, the Lady Sybilla, lived briefly at Tresmarrow and subsequent to the Restoration both of them died there. It was their favourite residence and at that period it was partly in South Petherwin parish and partly in St. Mary Magdalene parish. The Pipers chose to worship at St. Mary's, doubtless because it was a larger and more important church, better suited to their image than the village church of South Petherwin.

Tresmarrow remained the main seat of the Piper family until the family became extinct. It was strategically placed adjoining the main highway to Bodmin. Today small fragments of it remain incorporated in farm buildings there.

Honours were showered upon Sir Hugh. He married one Sybilla Parr of Exeter and lived in her house there for a while before going briefly to Tresmarrow and then back to Exeter. He returned permanently to Tresmarrow in 1660, when Charles II restored to him his estates and appointed him Lieut. Governor of the Citadel and Island of Plymouth, an important position. Charles was obviously deeply impressed because he also made Sir Hugh Captain of the Castle of Exeter, Constable of Launceston Castle and Warden of the Stannaries and finally he knighted him. What more could any man ask? But it did not end there. More honours were to come. Sir Hugh was appointed a Justice of the Peace for Cornwall and Devon, Alderman and representative in Parliament for Launceston (Dunheved) and when Charles II granted his Charter to Launceston in 1683 he made Sir Hugh the Deputy Recorder for life. Sir Hugh had estates at Egloskerry, Lawhitton, Lezant, Pipers Pool (named thus after him; was there once a lake or pool there?), South Petherwin, St. Clether, St. Thomas, Warbstow and Werrington. In the latter parish the farm now known as Peppers Hill was originally Pipers Hill and the name has been further perpetuated in a small estate of modern houses at Lady Cross, built in 1990 and named Peppers Hill Close. It is difficult these days to visualise one person, as opposed to the Duchy of Cornwall Estates, owning such vast areas of land and so many farms and estates.

Sir Hugh built Madford House in Launceston and was said to have been visited there by Charles I in 1644, when Charles was en route to fight Essex, the Parliamentarian General, at Braddock Down, near Lostwithiel. Charles had left his pregnant wife in Exeter and legend has it that she was very short of money to provide clothes and essential extra bedding for the forthcoming baby. Sir Hugh Piper is said to have melted down all his plate and sent its value to the Queen. No wonder he was rewarded with such a string of honours. Incidentally, the baby was born at Bamfylde House, Exeter in June 1644 and became Princess Henrietta.

Hugh Piper was also reputed to have entertained King Charles II. The house where he lived and received Charles I was destroyed by the Parliamentarians, when all Piper's estates and goods were seized following the defeat of the Royalists. As mentioned earlier, the estates were later returned to him by Charles II.

Sir Hugh Piper died in 1687 at the age of 76. A very ornate tomb was erected in St. Mary's Church to the memory of Sir Hugh and Lady Piper, on the spot where their own pew was situated. It remained in all its glory for many years and then one day in the 1920s one of the churchwardens noticed that the figures in the memorial were tilting. He pointed it out to the vicar but it was not thought to be serious. However, within a few days the whole memorial collapsed and lay as a pile of rubble on the floor. All that could be salvaged was the marble plaque and the figures of Sir High Piper and his wife kneeling at a prie Dieu. These relics may be seen on the right hand side as one descends the steps into the church.

There are other memorials in the church which repay close inspection. No one can fail to see the huge Piper cenotaph which has a somewhat curious story behind it.It was erected under the terms of the will of one Richard Wise, who had been employed by Granville Pyper, grandson of the famous Sir Hugh. The bond between the two men was so strong that it was to remain even in death, in the form of the florid memorial we see today. Wise left £500 for the purpose of building the memorial, and he also left specific instructions concerning its design. £500 bought a lot of craftsmanship in those days; one shudders to think what the cost would be today.

The cenotaph was designed after the style of Inigo Jones and was crowned by busts of the two men, bewigged and dignified. The story behind it is, to say the least, unconventional. There was a certain amount of controversy among church members at the time about the erection of the memorial. Richard Wise and Granville Pyper were both buried in Bath. Pyper had died there but Wise died in Launceston and left a request that his ashes be buried in Bath beside his friend. Despite controversy over the then unusual request and the even more controversial erection of a memorial, in 1720 the Corporation granted a licence for the cenotaph to be erected. It is ornately created in

THE CHURCH SCENE

Part of the ornate Pyper-Wise cenotaph in St. Mary Magdalene Church.

variously coloured marbles and incorporates the figures of Faith, Hope and Charity. It also incorporates the Pyper coat of arms, three magpies. The arms are said to be thus because magpies are great chatterers and fighters among their kind as well as being builders of secure nests, all Piper traits. Incidentally, the Piper cenotaph was protected by iron railings at its base until 1852 and now has a marble tablet from Sir Hugh Piper's memorial placed in front of it - a bit of a hotch potch of family history. It is sited near where the Piper pew was situated.

And the change of spelling in the family name? Simply keeping up with the Joneses! In the reign of Queen Anne it became fashionable to change an 'i' into a 'y' in surnames; considered more elegant, one supposes. From then on the Pipers (as well as that other well-known Cornish family, the Vivians) signed their names with a 'y'. The two families were united when one of Sir Hugh Piper's grandsons married a Vivian (Vyvyan) and they lived at Madford, Launceston, a mansion built by Sir Hugh.

The Pipers distinguished themselves in Launceston in a number of ways. One Piper joined with another William Wise (not the cenotaph man) and successfully raised a militia regiment in the town to subdue the Papists. One Digory Piper gained fame as a pirate with the notorious Sir John Killigrew of Falmouth. He also was a Launceston lad but his exploits meant that he was less remembered in the town than his illustrious relatives. Even his burial place is unknown today. Past generations did not suffer scapegraces gladly.

Another colourful Launceston family with memorials in St. Mary's Church were the Chings. They were a somewhat flamboyant self-made family who came into prominence in the town in 1724 and their stature grew enormously when in 1726 John Ching patented a worm lozenge and it made him a fortune. All through the ages money has talked! John Ching even opened a shop in Cheapside, London. In those days people took worm lozenges just as folk take aspirins today and they were quite a money spinner. The lozenges were advertised as "the best medicine in the world" (no trading standards officers in those days) and sold like hot cakes. King George III was reputed to have taken them but their image was somewhat dented after it was recorded that a child died as a

THE CHURCH SCENE

result of swallowing them. As with today's medication, an overdose was obviously not advisable.

However, the product maintained its popularity and after John died his widow continued marketing the pills and even took out a patent in 1808 for an improved formula. Soon afterwards, however, she relinquished the London shop and a partner who had been in business with her took it over. Rebecca bought a splendid house in Broad Street, Launceston, originally built for a judge and having a carriage entrance through the house to the yard beyond.

John Ching of lozenge fame had a son called Thomas, who was in business as a chemist in both Launceston and Stratton. He and his son John were the first people in the area to take an interest in cricket, said to be a game new to the district and introduced by a builder from the Midlands who was working on the rebuilding of Trebursye House.

Thomas Ching was mayor of the town in 1836 but died soon after completing his term of office. His son John was also a chemist and a tea and wine merchant as well; he carried on the family tradition by being mayor of the town on three separate occasions. He took a Mr Wise as a partner in his chemist's business and this author's grandfather, Frederick Culley, was apprenticed to Mr Wise at the start of the young man's career, studying to become a physician.

John Ching was a very public spirited person: he organised the Launceston Fire Brigade and in 1852 presented the fine reredos which we see in St. Mary's Church today. At that time the church was being rebuilt in the period of Victorian frenzy of church rebuilding and 'restoration' which, far from enhancing, totally ruined many ancient Cornish churches. Fortunately St. Mary's was not treated too badly. John Ching died at his home, Hendra, Dunheved Road, Launceston in 1883.

Both Thomas and John Ching suffered tragedies in their families. A small brass memorial in the church records the sad death of Thomas Procter Ching, son of Thomas and his wife Sarah (nee Procter). His end was tragic. As a midshipman in H.M.S. "Eaton" he sailed for China via Sydney in 1834 but his ship was wrecked on the notorious Great Barrier Reef off Australia. Only four of the crew escaped in a boat and reached Batavia in the Dutch East Indies; natives murdered the remaining twenty seven people, including Thomas Ching who, along with the others, was eaten by cannibals. Several generations of Launceston children have irreverently referred to young Thomas Ching as "Eton, Eaton, Eaten Ching". This was inspired by the curious chain of events which led to him being educated at Eton College, sailing in H.M.S. "Eaton" and finally being eaten by cannibals.

John Ching's youngest son Henry was also a midshipman in the Royal Navy and he died of yellow fever in Jamaica in 1863. He is commemorated in a stained glass window, erected in the church as the gift of the officers and crew of H.M.S. "Shannon", in which he was serving at the time, as a token of their regard for him.

Another Ching carrying on the naval tradition in the family was Capt Lawrence Ching, R.N., who died in 1911 and the family gave the small terracotta statuette of St. Mary Magdalene which is in the niche over the church porch. Today it is often regarded by older residents of the town as a memorial to the Ching family.

There have been other interesting features of the religious scene in Launceston over the years. For instance, who remembers ever hearing stories about John Murlin, the "weeping prophet"? Murlin was born in Launceston in 1772 and is described as having "a godless youth" and being known as a "cursing, drunken farmer" before his conversion. John Wesley's visits to the area brought about his conversion and he became so powerful in the pulpit that Wesley invited him to become a circuit preacher and sent him to West Cornwall. He was known as "the weeping prophet" because whilst delivering his sermons he would weep tears of joy and religious fervour. He had a long career as an evangelist, although in his latter years he suffered considerable ill health and physical infirmity. When he died at the age of 77 he was accorded the greatest honour of being interred in Wesley's tomb at the Methodist "cathedral" in City Road, London.

The Baptist church in Launceston also had at one time a large following and on a Sunday in the first week of September 1880 a public baptism took place at Polson Bridge, when three persons were baptised and it was reported that there was a large crowd of spectators.

Who knows today where a religious sect called The Exclusives had their chapel in Race Hill? We know they had one because "The Launceston Weekly News" of 12th September 1891 reported that John Webber of South Petherwin slipped and fell 18 feet to the ground whilst at work on a scaffolding at the chapel being erected in Race Hill, Launceston for the Exclusives. Incidentally, he survived but was reported to be "very much bruised".

Today the Salvation Army is a very highly respected and popular religious organisation which does a tremendous amount of good for the poor and

THE CHURCH SCENE

needy but it was not always so. On 9th February 1884 the "Launceston Weekly News" reported that "Launceston Salvationists were followed on Tuesday evening by a yelling mob but the presence of several policemen prevented any actual collision. On Thursday a violent and disgraceful attack was made on the Salvationists in Westgate Street by the young men of Launceston". There were hooligans and 'yobbos' in those days just as today but, thankfully, nowadays the religious life of the town can proceed peacefully, with all denominations going about their worship uninterrupted.

This gravestone is believed to be unique in Cornwall and possibly in the country. The deceased was a Freemason and not only are Freemasonry symbols carved at the top, but also the wording and epitaph incorporate Freemasonry "language".

CHAPTER 3
Money, Money, Money!

The old word 'moneyer', meaning an authorised coiner of money, has almost disappeared from the English language, because modern technology makes it obsolete: the director and workers at the Royal Mint at Llantrisant hardly come into the same category.

However, at one time the moneyer was a very important person in Launceston or, to be more precise, in St. Stephens. Thoughts of his role have been brought back to mind in recent years when an application from the Church Commissioners to build a new vicarage in the enclosure known as Mint Field at St. Stephens was rejected because the Cornwall Archaeological Unit, the official County Council organisation, feels that important archaeological remains may be hidden beneath the soil and proposes at some time to conduct a 'dig', using the latest seeking equipment in the hope of discovering more about a period of Launceston's history about which at present only sketchy details are known.

We do know that back in Saxon times the Canons of St. Stephen had a priory at what we now know as St. Stephens and indeed in recent times burials in a part of the modern extension to the churchyard have been halted because grave digging operations revealed fragments of walls which are the remains of that priory and which will also, perhaps, in due course, be excavated. We have already seen in an earlier chapter how St. Stephens was at one time an important market centre. It is therefore logical to suppose that the mint was part of the widespread operations of the Canons of St. Stephen. The Domesday Book confirms this. Launceston (spelt very differently then) was in those days a 'simple borough', i.e. one owned entirely by one person, and the Canons of St. Stephen were classed as one person for Domesday purposes. They are also recorded as having a mint in Saxon and Norman times.

Experts claim that as far as is known Launceston was the only place in Cornwall to have the privilege of a mint and furthermore its coinage was not just for use in Cornwall, it circulated in all parts of the country.

Coins issued from the Launceston mint comprised the reigns of Ethelred II, William I, William II, Henry I, Stephen and Henry II. At first they bore the word 'LANSTF', later 'STEFANI' and finally 'LANST' to denote their town of origin.

The earliest coin which can with any degree of certainty be attributed to a Cornish place of mintage actually came from St. Stephens and is a unique silver penny produced in the reign of King Ethelred II (979-1016). It is now almost priceless but on 23rd November 1895 it was sold by Messrs Sotheby, Wilkinson & Hodge for just £4.7.6, having passed through two famous numismatic collections and having gained a slightly higher price each time it was sold! Historic objects were obviously not valued as much in the past as they are now.

This first coin from Launceston bore a diademed bust of the king on the obverse and the legend + BRVN M-O LANSF. which, translated, shows one Brun as the name of the moneyer and Lansf. the place of coinage. From this it is presumed that the Saxon name for Launceston was Lanstefanton, meaning 'the town of the Church of St. Stephen'. As an aside to that, it should be noted that most of the early historians invariably used the termination 'don' or 'dun' meaning hill, rather than 'ton' or 'tun' meaning town, but that is a somewhat vexed argument which will probably rumble on for ever.

Incidentally, there was a moneyer named Brun coining at Exeter in the same type of coinage and 'Bruna' is on several coins from the Lydford mint,

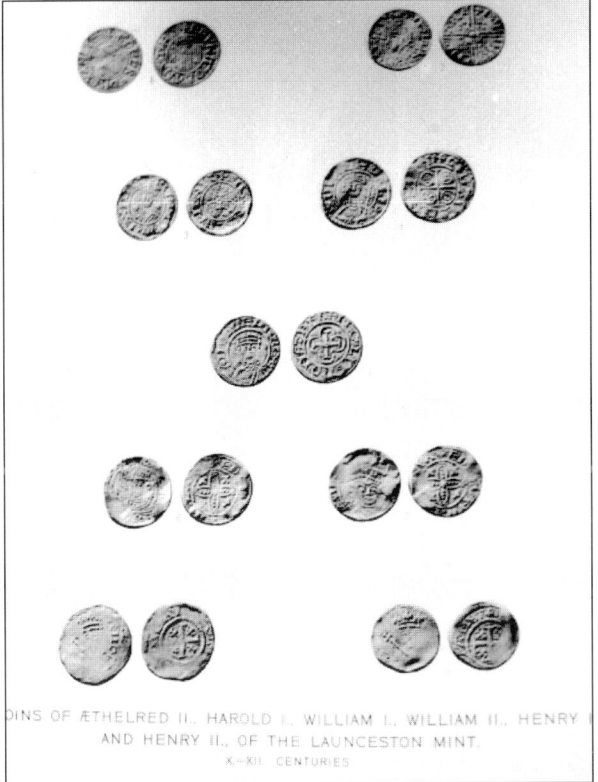

Coins from the Launceston Mint.

so the name was probably the Saxon equivalent of 'John' today, a very popular Christian name.

The moneyers' names were perpetuated in the same families and the moneyer's craft was a somewhat closely guarded art. Even in those days there was a danger of counterfeiters getting to work! Most of the names of the moneyers were of Danish or Saxon origin. Launceston moneyers' names appearing on coins also included Ieglier, Godric and Goric. Incidentally, the Pipe Rolls of Henry II contain an account of the Launceston Mint, showing that it was pretty important in its day.

It is believed by numismatic experts that a mint existed at St. Stephen even before the time of King Ethelred but to date no definite evidence has come to light.

Records appertaining to the Launceston mint are fragmentary but the next coin believed to have come from there was a silver penny of the reign of Harold I, who succeeded his father Canute in 1035. It is something of an enigma, as the experts cannot prove that it comes from Launceston at all, yet the indications are that it was a St. Stephens 'issue'. The mint name appears to be given as LANZTE and the moneyer's name as Gawine, which, incidentally, is a name more usually associated with the Arthurian legend, spelt as 'Gawaine'.

The coins of William I which came from the St. Stephens Mint are not appreciably different in design from those issued during the reigns of earlier kings. The eminent numismatist P. W. P. Carlyon-Britten wrote in "The British Numismatic Journal" in 1906 that several specimens of the Conquerer's coins from the Launceston mint were in existence and he dated them between September 1077 and September 1080. He also stated that they bore the words "Sasoti Stefani" and pointed out that they were unusual in that the words were in Latin, whereas all later types of the reigns of William I and William II (better known as William Rufus) carried the name of the moneyer followed by the word 'ON', meaning 'of' or 'in', and lastly the somewhat abbreviated name of the mint town. Mr Carlyon-Britten goes on to inform that the dies were probably engraved in London, on the written instructions of the then Dean of St. Stephens, proving that Cornwall was by no means cut off from the rest of the country.

Indeed, of the first type of William II coins from St. Stephens, a specimen was found as far away as Shillington in Bedfordshire, which showed that they circulated widely and were not merely Cornish currency. That coin again gave prominence, in abbreviated mint letters, to the principal name, 'Stephen' but with the accession of Henry II in the 1150s things changed and it became the custom to give enough of the first part of the place name to ensure its identification, so back they went to the word 'Lanst' on the coins, almost the same as on the coinage of Ethelred II.

So what happened after the reign of Henry II as far as the St Stephens mint was concerned? That we do not know. It apparently closed down but no records exist to indicate closure, reason for closure and intended closure. We are left wondering 'why?'. Such an apparently flourishing and important institution disappearing into oblivion without any explanation allows the imagination to run riot. We can put forward all manner of theories but we shall probably never know now; perhaps excavations at some later date will reveal an answer to the mystery.

Meanwhile, here mention may be made of a fanciful theory put forward in the 1870s by another eminent numismatist, Sir John Evans. He claimed that some coins of Edward the Confessor were minted at Newport, "a borough in the county of Cornwall, adjoining that of Launceston". He put forward some extraordinary reasons for reaching this conclusion, summarily disposing of the claims of seven other and far more likely places of the

MONEY, MONEY, MONEY!

name of Newport to have the privilege of possessing a mint. Since Newport did not officially exist at the time of Edward the Confessor it seems that Sir John was indulging in a little fantasy but for years his theories on this matter were taken seriously during the last century. We are reminded of an old northcountry saying - "there's nowt so strange as folks"!

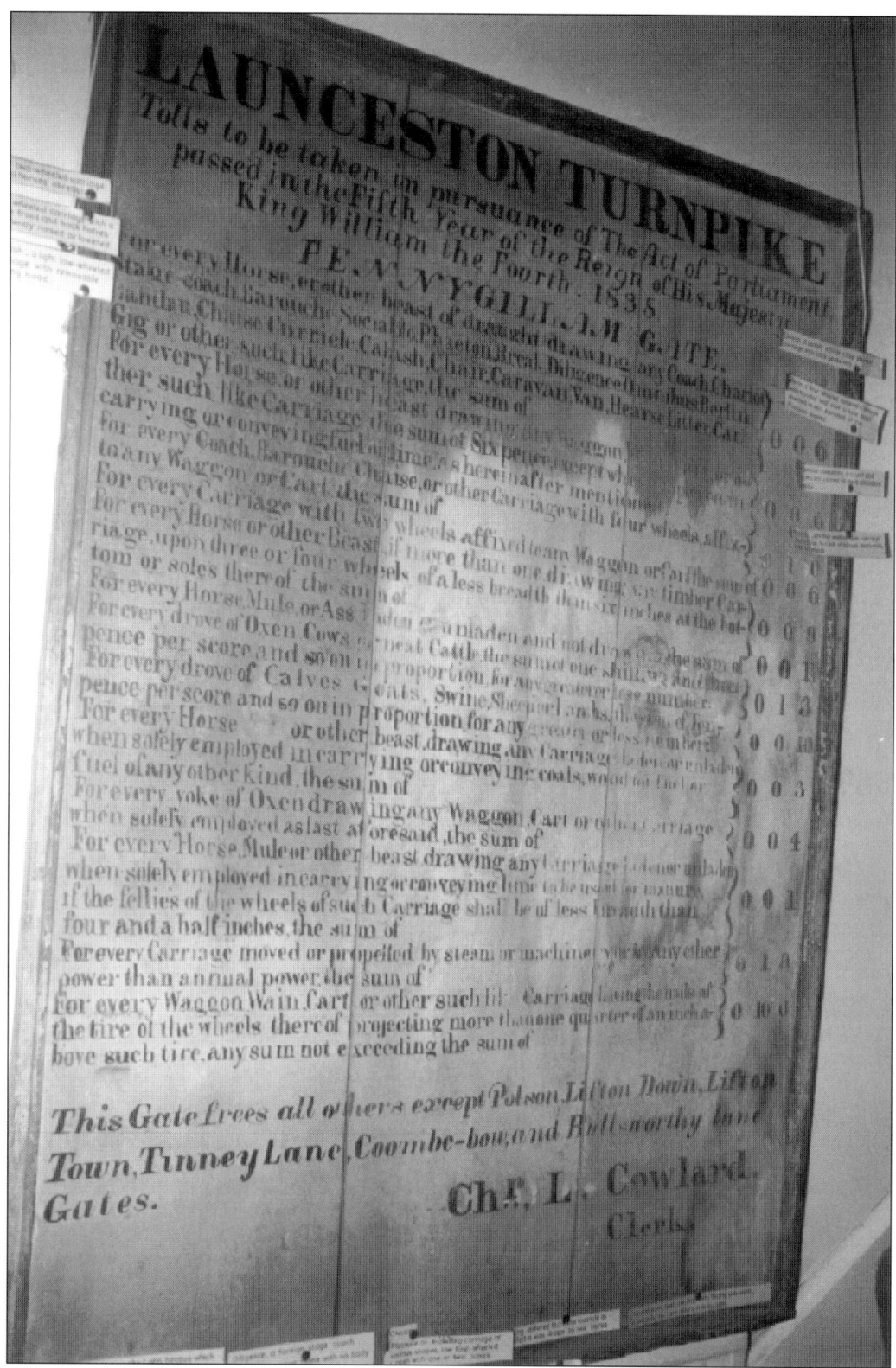

CHAPTER 4
Launceston's Turnpike Trust

When we travel the roads around Launceston today we do so without hindrance but it was not always that way. The idea of levying a toll to finance the upkeep of roads dates from the fourteenth century but turnpike roads date only from 1663.

Turnpike Trusts were formed to administer certain roads or groups of roads and were empowered to levy tolls and borrow money on the security of the tolls which they raised. The trusts were mainly formed by local authorities to meet the particular needs of their area and although regulated by Parliament, they were never controlled by Whitehall. Areas with the greatest amount of traffic had turnpike roads first and so the south east introduced them before other parts of England but they soon spread throughout the country. They did not reach Cornwall and Devon until the mid eighteenth century, mainly because the population in those counties was sparse and wheeled traffic scarce.

A General Turnpike Act passed in 1773 made it easier to set up a turnpike trust but by that time many were already established and Launceston was no exception. The turnpike roads around Launceston followed the line of already existing roads and duties of the trusts were mainly concerned with improving the roads to a standard suitable for wheeled traffic as opposed to packhorse traffic only, and maintaining them. An Elizabethan system of maintaining roads by statute labour on a parish basis was still followed to a certain extent in the Launceston area. The Turnpike Trustees were also responsible for building tollhouses and acquiring land for that purpose and it was sometimes like Compulsory Purchase Orders today, with objectors just as vocal and protesting as they often are today when new highways are planned.

If a toll collector (or toll gatherer as the Launceston employees were known) lived close to where a toll gate was situated he was merely provided with a flimsy shelter. All tollhouses had to display a board detailing charges, and other requirements were a lamp and obviously, a gate or chain, these being statutory equipment. Toll gatherers were either paid wages or were self employed persons who 'tendered' for the job and hoped to make a living from the tolls. In the case of Launceston it would appear that the toll gatherers were employed by the Turnpike Trust, which kept a close eye on their activities.

Travelling on the turnpike roads was not cheap. Each trust set its own tolls, according to the length of roads which it had to keep in repair and the amount of traffic using them. The number of wheels on a vehicle or the number of horses drawing it affected the price chargeable for a vehicle, as well as the type of 'cargo' being carried.

Like the Launceston market tolls, the turnpike tolls make interesting reading, for absolutely nothing was overlooked: every type of traffic and eventuality was catered for in the scale of charges. The original board listing charges at the Pennygillam gate in Launceston in 1835 can now be seen in the town's Lawrence House Museum. Charges quoted are as follows:-

For every Horse, or other beast of draught drawing any Coach, Chariot, Stage Coach, Barouch, Sociable, Phaeton, Breal, Diligence, Omnibus, Berlin, Laundau, Chaise, Curricle, Calash, Chair, Caravan, Van, Hearse, Litter Car, Gig or other such like Carriage, the sum of 0 0 6
For every Horse, other beast drawing any Waggon, Wain, Cart or another such like Carriage, the sum of Sixpence, except when employed in carrying or conveying fuel or lime as hereinafter mentioned 0 0 6
For every Coach, Barouche, Chaise or other

Carriage with four wheels, affix to any Waggon or Cart, the sum of 0 1 0
For every Carriage with two wheels affixed to any Waggon or Cart the sum of 0 0 6
For every Horse or other Beast, if more than one, drawing any Timber Carriage, upon three or four wheels of a less breadth than six inches at the bottom or soles thereof the sum of 0 0 9
For every Horse, Mule or Ass laden or unladen and not drawing, the sum of 0 0 1½
For every drove of Oxen, Cows or neat Cattle the sum of one shilling and threepence per score and so on in proportion, for any greater or less number 0 1 3
For every drove of Calves, Goats, Swine, Sheep or Lambs, the sum of tenpence per score and so on in proportion for any greater or less number 0 0 10
For every Horse or other beast, drawing any Carriage, laden or unladen when solely employed in carrying or conveying coals, wood for fuel, or fuel of any other kind, the sum of 0 0 3
For every Yoke of Oxen drawing any Waggon, Cart or other Carriage when solely employed as last aforesaid, the sum of 0 0 4
For every Horse, Mule or other beast drawing any Carriage laden or unladen when solely employed in carrying or conveying lime to be used for manure, if the fellies of the wheels of such Carriage shall be of less breadth than four and a half inches, the sum of 0 0 1
For every Carriage moved or propelled by steam or machinery or by any other power than annual power, the sum of 0 1 0
For every Waggon, Wain, Cart or other such like Carriage having the nails of the tire of the wheels thereof projecting more than one quarter of an inch above such tire, any sum not exceeding the sum of 0 10 0

The board went on to announce that "This Gate frees all others except Polson, Lifton Down, Lifton Town, Tinney Lane, Coombe-bow, and Bullsworthy Lane Gates" and it was signed 'Ch^r, L. Cowlard, Clerk.'

It would appear that the mention of 'annual' power should have read 'animal' power and the names of some of the forms of transport seem very strange, even unknown, today. A Diligence was a foreign stage coach; a Sociable, an open carriage with facing side seats or a tricycle for two riders side by side; a Calash was a light low-wheeled carriage with removable folding hood; a Chariot a stately vehicle or for turnpike purposes, a four-wheeled vehicle with back seats only; a Berlin was a four-wheeled covered carriage with a hooded seat and said to have been invented in 1660, a product of the Prussian capital.

The Launceston Turnpike Trust was formed in 1760 and the first meeting of Trustees was held at the Guild Hall on Tuesday, 17th June 1760, for "widening and keeping in repair several roads leading to the Borough of Launceston". The list of the first trustees makes fascinating reading and over the years many well-known Launceston names of the past appear as being appointed trustees. At the first meeting they were headed by John Carpenter, the mayor at that time, and others were Edmund Cheyne, Joshua Thomas, Richard Welsh, Richard Bennett, Ascott Bickford, William Carpenter, George Fursdon, Joseph Hodges, Joseph Hales, Arthur Kelly, Richard Kingdon, John Lethbridge, George Mann, John Sawle, Richard Vyvyan, Christopher Watkins, Charles Bedford, Philip Welsh and Thomas Welsh. Each name was carefully segregated to show the particular gentleman's status in society, i.e. 'Gent', 'Esqre' or 'Clerk'.

It is amusing to note from the minutes of that first meeting that the trustees adjourned to the Kings Arms, presumably to refresh themselves after their exhausting deliberations! Business dealt with at the first meeting was the provision of 'Chains and Bars and Ropes at Polson Bridge, Chapple, a Stop Gate at Windmill Lane leading from Westgate Street, two at Pages Cross, two or more at St. Stephens, one at Dutson Cross, one or more at graves and mills'. The latter seems rather curious. It was agreed that wages for tollkeepers should be 5/- per week. Surveyors were appointed for the roads and these were Samuel Dunn - Northgate to Yeolmbridge, Westgate to Pennygillam Pool and Southgate to Pages Cross; John Harris - White Horse at Newport to Newbridge. It was decided that each toll gatherer had to take his accounts to each meeting to be inspected and approved and also to notify any damage.

The acquiring of land proved just as thorny a problem then as it is today. One decision at the first trustees' meeting was that 'Agent of the Bishop of Exeter be paid £1.2.8 for land taken out of the field near Polson Bridge where the Tollhouse stands'.

Most of the meetings in the early years dealt with finance - borrowing, wages and salaries. On 5th December 1760 it was decided that the road at the bottom of Angel Hill be repaired and 17/6 paid for land at Chapple. One 6th April 1761 it was resolved that 'none of the Surveyors employed by the Trustees give more than 7/- a week to the

LAUNCESTON'S TURNPIKE TRUST

The Dutson (top), St. Stephens (middle) and Town Mills Toll Houses as they are today.

labourers to be employed on the turnpike roads'.

Coryndon Carpenter, famed in Launceston for building Eagle House on, so the story goes, the strength of winning £10,000 in a lottery, was added to the list of trustees in 1761. On Wednesday, 30th September 1761 business dealt with was 'Quarries at Windmill to be railed off' and it was also announced that William Turner had built the tollhouses and tollgates at St. Stephens and Dutson, both of which are still in existence and still lived in. He was paid in instalments to the sum of £500.

John Harris of Hayne, Stowford, and Humphrey Lawrence of Launceston both joined the Trustees in 1762 and they were among those who were appointed to examine all the roads to ensure that they were properly finished before money was paid for their construction. In the same year Hugh Taylor was fined 50/- for assaulting the tollgatherer at St. Stephens Gate but later one guinea was returned to him, for what reason we do not know. Samuel Dunn was paid 6/6 per yard for repairing the road from South Petherwin Churchtown to the Green beyond Tregiller (sic) Lane End and Honiton Lane End, and for Pennygillam Gate to the Barn. Samuel Dunn was awarded several contracts by the trustees, so his work was obviously approved. He was also employed to 'clear up the drain and gutter on the several roads belonging to the Turnpike'.

By 1763 claims for compensation were beginning to come in. On 16th May that year Mrs Catherine Manning was given 43/8 for damage done to her field near Pages Cross and the road from Kenners (sic) House (a Kenner was a watchman) to Pypers (sic) Pool seemed to cause a lot of trouble.

Meetings were frequently adjourned because not enough trustees were present, so they do not appear to have taken their appointments too seriously.

On 30th May 1764 the trustees "contracted with Bartholomew Hore for making the road from Northern end of Yeolmbridge to Lady Cross in the parish of Werrington and from Tiphill Lane in Werrington aforesaid". The latter was presumably the original name for Tipple Lane which today forms a junction with the main Launceston-Holsworthy road in the parish of St. Giles-in-the-Heath. Frequent repairs were required on the road from St. Stephens Down to Egloskerry Church Town, whilst some other roads appeared to require little or no maintenance.

One 14th November 1764 the urgent business was "That the marsh or hollow under the House on Hallworthy Down commonly called Cold Northcott be forthwith repaired." John Harris, labourer, of the parish of Illogan, was given the task of repairing the hollow and it seems strange that someone from far away in west Cornwall should be given the job when there must have been plenty of local labour available. Perhaps he tendered lowest for the work. John Harris was later appointed Surveyor for some roads.

Claims for compensation began to escalate. In the winter of 1764 the trustees were called upon to examine damage done to Mr John Carpenter's and Mr William Edwards's fields near Peters Finger by digging for stone there to make the roads.

Some names of lands in use in those days have now disappeared. On 6th June 1765 notice was given for making the road from Horrells Gate in Werrington to the next water beyond Stondaller Lane in North Petherwin. No one is quite clear today where Stondaller Lane is or was located.

The Trustees were by now incurring considerable expense in settling claims for compensation. Either landowners were getting wise to the fact that they could be on to a good thing or the Trustees were becoming more bold and not taking much account of people's feelings or property. In 1765 William Gynn was paid one guinea for damage to his fields at Tresmarrow and William Lampey received 10/- for damage to his fields at Netherbridge. Costs were also mounting for the upkeep of roads. On 4th July 1765 Bartholomew Hore was paid the balance of his accounts for making roads from Lawhitton Cross to Greston (sic) Bridge, from Yeolmbridge to Lady Cross and from Dobles Thorn to Peters Finger and he was also discharged from being surveyor of those roads. It will be seen that the extent of the area for which the Launceston Turnpike Trustees were responsible was much greater than the Borough of Launceston today, and extended to such outlying parishes as Broadwoodwidger and Lewtrenchard in the south and Red Post in the north.

In 1766 attention was being paid to the statute labour situation and on 19th March that year a list was drawn up of 'inhabitants liable to do statute Labour' and also prepared were lists of 'their several roads within their several parishes, the following parts and proportions of the Statute Labour to be done on the Turnpike roads by the said parishes'. The proportion given for Werrington was one sixth part, that for Lezant one fortieth part, Egloskerry one twentieth part, North Petherwin one thirty sixth part, St Giles-in-the-Heath one sixth part, etc.

A decision in October 1767 that "a Tollhouse or Tollgate, Bars or six Chains be erected at a prominent place between Thomas Doyle's house at Lifton and Tinney Bridge" was reversed two months later as "the Surveyor reported there was not a convenient place for building a Tollhouse or Tollgates". That year the Trustees "contracted with John Harris to make the road Haggadon (sic) Green to Sitcott at 6/6, of Parish Statute Measure which is to be formed 20ft. wide and stoned, furzed and gravelled 16ft. wide and finished by Ladyday next".

Weekly meetings were arranged from 1769 but were mostly adjourned because insufficient number of Trustees was present.

Mention was made earlier of the extent of the Turnpike Trust's liability and the following parishes were run by it:- Treneglos, Laneast, Lawhitton, South Petherwin, Egloskerry, Lewtrenchard, Marystow, Boyton, Werrington, Stowford, St. Giles-in-the-Heath, St. Cleather (sic), Lifton, Lezant, St. Thomas, St. Mary Magdalene, St. Stephens, North Petherwin, Thruselton and Trewen; just about approximate to the Launceston postal district today!

It would appear that in the early years of the Turnpike Trust cheating was not uncommon. Presumably there was some opposition to paying to travel on roads which had previously offered free access, even though the Turnpike Trust greatly improved those roads and it also provided employment for a number of people. Once the roads had become established it would seem that "doing" the Trustees was quite an accepted practice in the parishes. For instance, on 5th March 1772 the Clerk was instructed to "enforce his Summons against the Surveyors of the Parish of Maristow to attend at the next meeting to show cause why the penalty of £5 should not be levied on them for their neglect in not returning a Perfect List of all Persons liable to do their Statute Labour in the said parish". Then on 6th April the following year Thomas Westlake was summoned to appear before the Trustees at the next meeting "to show cause why he shall not be proceeded against for delivering to the said Trustees at a former meeting a false List of the Inhabitants of the Parish of Laneast liable to do Statute Labour on Launceston Turnpike" and on 5th June they were "fined according to the Directions of the Act for delivering upon Oath a false list". The amount of the fine is not known.

Around this time complaints were flying on both sides. The Trustees ordered "Mr Edward Brendon be applied to by the Clerk to remove the Saw Pit Timber which is a very great nuisance on the Road leading to Grestone Bridge" whilst Mr George Borlase made a complaint that a Committee appointed at an earlier meeting had not "proceeded to view the Damage done to his Estate by making the Turnpike Road leading from Chapple Gate to South Petherwin". Mr Borlase was paid £5 compensation. There was a summons issued to men from Lanteglos for evading the Toll at St. Stephens Turnpike Gate and they were ordered to attend the next meeting of the Trustees. Then in 1780 John Facey complained against Solomon Spettigue, Gent. "for having contracted with another for the sum of £1.11.6 in order to obtain tickets for passing through the several Toll Gates contrary to the Act". Shady business against the Trust was obviously not confined to the lower strata of society! Mr Spettigue was also ordered to appear before the Trustees. Their job was not an enviable one. Despite fines and reprimands by the Trustees, cheating still continued. The next move was "A person to stand at the Workhouse every Saturday with a Chain or Rope across the Road in order to find out any Imposition upon the Trust".

At no time did the Trust seem to be without its difficulties and its relations with the public were hardly cordial. It is quite obvious, in fact, that both sides hated each other. Right through the 19th century there were constant complaints, both from the public against the Turnpike Trust and from the Trust against the public. It was not only the less well to do who tried to cheat the Trust. The Rev'd John Bradon of Stowford received a summons for non payment of tolls at Lifton Stop Gate and in 1786 there was quite a scandal when Mr Hales, Clerk to the Trustees, is recorded as not having paid in the balance of money due to the Trustees. Mr Hales was threatened with dismissal and then prosecution and then prison, but before the worst could happen someone stood surety for him. Then in 1817 Mr Richard Cope was proposed as a Trustee but the election was postponed because he was a "dissenting Minister and a Nonconformist" and in the spring of that year one William Royle submitted a written objection to Mr Cope, declaring "his election illegal because of him being a dissenting Minister and a Nonconformist and considered ineligible to fill such a place of Trust". Nevertheless, Mr Cope finally took the oath as a Trustee.

One of the saddest aspects of the period of the Turnpike Trust was the number of animals killed in connection with Turnpike activities. In May 1809 Thomas Pethick was awarded £7 compensation for the loss of his horse which fell over Crockadillett Quarry in the parish of St. Thomas; in January 1812 John Cowland was awarded £7 for the loss of his horse which fell over the Quarry at Kenners

House and on 14th July 1818 Thomas Pethick lost yet another horse at Berry Down Quarry, near Tregadillett, but that time he was given only £5 in compensation. One can only assume that Thomas Pethick was a very careless and/or incompetent waggoner.

As the 19th century progressed so did the Trust's methods become more sophisticated. In November 1809 the Clerk was instructed to make enquiries "as to the Expense of erecting Weighing Engines" and in January 1810 he was instructed to write to Sharp & Co. to enquire expense of a Weighing Engine and "to learn the expense of erecting the vault to receive the same and other incidental charges". Strangely, there is no record of a Weighing Engine ever being installed or even of the estimated cost.

Mail coaches did not pay tolls but in 1811 there was an idea that "the Mail Coaches will at some future day be subject to payment of tolls".

In 1840 the meetings of the Trustees, which had always been held at the Guildhall, moved to the White Hart Inn and were held there until December 1841, when they were moved again, that time to the Central Subscription Rooms, where they were held for the remaining period of the Turnpike Trust.

However, the end was approaching. In July 1879 the Surveyor was instructed to have the several gates removed on 1st November at cost not exceeding £1.0.0 and the Clerk was ordered to remind the lessees that their tenancies ceased at 12 o'clock noon on 1st November. In July that year Mr Ching reported to the Trustees on what offers he had received for the toll houses and frontages; they were not enormous. Richard Mitchell of St. Stephens offered £75 for the Dutson toll house, Col. Deakin offered £40 for Pages Cross, £50 was the offer from Mr White for Polson but James Treleaven offered only £5 for Lifton Down and Mr Reed was even more stingy with his £3 offer for St. Thomas Bridge house. The Duke of Bedford was prepared to pay £10 for Dobles Thorne and Mr Bradshaw offered £10 for Lifton Down, a paltry total of £185 for all of them.

Also on offer was "the box at Hurle Lane on the Bude road together with the toll board and Post". No remnants of any tollboxes have survived but at what is now the junction of Horrell Lane, Werrington with the B3254 Launceston-Bude road the spot where the tollbox stood can still clearly be identified. Although the junction has been widened in modern times and was obviously altered when the B3254 road was constructed, the line of the original hedge, curved and with a handsome oak tree forming part of it, is still in situ.

It must be borne in mind that the Duke of Northumberland gave land for a new road from Yeolmbridge to Bude in 1833. The old road ran along between the barrows from Wringsdown turn to Red Post. It went from Newport, up St. Stephens Hill to Barricadoes gate, then via Castle Hill plantation to Yeolmbridge, then Wringsdown to what is now Horrell Cross. The line of it, flanked by trees, is still clearly visible from the B3254 road, running from a field gate opposite the junction of the Egloskerry-B3254 roads towards Yeolmbridge, and of course it is still a thoroughfare from Yeolmbridge to Horrell Cross, with at Wringsdown some of the original cottages beside it still lived in and with the façades unmodernised.

The final meeting of the Trustees was held at The Central Subscription Rooms on 2nd March 1880. The last chairman was Mr W. T. May and the last Trustees were John Archer, Charles Gurney, W. W. Martyn, C. G. Archer, John Ching and A. M. Harvey. The chairman signed the necessary cheques for distributing the balance of the Trust's accounts among the several Highways Boards entitled to it and the Clerk was directed to take charge of the books and papers and other effects belonging to the Trust. Col Archer proposed a final vote of thanks to the chairman and it was all over - the turnpike roads had faded into history.

The local population had rejoiced long before then and on 6th November 1879 "The West Briton" newspaper gleefully reported "The church bells were rung at Launceston on Saturday in recognition of the fact that at midday the turnpike tolls in the district ceased to exist. Market people, as a rule, 'came late' in order to escape paying on the last day". The newspaper went on to report that the Trust had paid its debt of £10,000 in two years and some months under the prescribed time, and that the tolls had been let at £1,900 during the last two years, as compared with the sum of £1,400 when the roads opened, thus, claimed the paper, showing the great increase in the amount of traffic over the Trust's road.

And so another chapter of Launceston's history ended. Now in 1991 the town has seen its first traffic lights - at Newport. Will the by-pass ever become a toll road, thus turning the clock back to the infamous days of the Turnpike Trust? Only time will tell.

CHAPTER 5
Rip Roaring Launceston!

Those who today mourn the changing face of Launceston, who point to such disagreeable features as noisy motor cycles being ridden aimlessly and endlessly around the town centre in the evenings; often less than salubrious hippies congregating in the Square, and rowdiness when the town's public houses and similar establishments close for the night, perhaps do not realise that the town was not always the peaceful, quiet place they would like to think it was before the present century and that equally repugnant goings on occurred in the past, albeit of a somewhat different nature, and they, too, were condemned by peace loving and respectable citizens.

In the mining boom of the 19th century Launceston was not an exception. In fact, the area was much involved. Perhaps the oldest activity in that field in the area was that at the Higher Truscott Mine; a copper sett there was granted by Edward Herle to George Kingdon in 1718 and a clause in the deed forbids the destruction of "any shafts belonging to the said work", which indicates underground mining having taken place before 1718. It produced high grade copper. At Badgall the Baron Mine, named after the Baron family of Tregeare, became famous for the discovery of gold and silver - although before anyone gets excited about that it must be stated that only twenty-six pennyweights of silver to one ton of ore, and seventeen pennyweights four grammes of fine gold to the ton were ever found there.

But there *is* gold in the neighbourhood - or so some people thought at the time! - because in November 1893 a syndicate was formed for working the Fernhill Gold Reefs at Lifton and in December that year a London newspaper reported that gold-bearing reefs on the Fernhill Estate, near Launceston, were being tested. Unfortunately there appear to be no further references to this exciting project, so presumably it was not successful in its quest.

There was also mining in other parts of St. Stephens and the parishes of Lawhitton, Lewannick, Lezant, North Hill, South Petherwin, Tremaine and Tresmeer and also at Trebursye.

So the miners came to town in Launceston and ensured that it was the "swinging capital of Cornwall" of its day.

In the 1830s and '40s it was recorded that there were up to forty public houses in the town and although the numbers appear to have dropped rapidly after the 1840s, there were at least fifteen public houses in the town about one hundred and thirty years ago, and this figure did not include what were called beer and cider houses. These rather more 'down-market' establishments mostly kept open all night but they did close at midnight on Saturdays and reopened at midnight on Sundays in deference to the wishes of those who wanted to keep the Sabbath sacred. There were ale and cider houses (or shops, as they were often known) at Chapple, Western Road, Westgate, Race Hill, Angel Hill, High Street, Northgate Street, the then Fore Street, Tower Street, St. Thomas Hill, North Road, Southgate and St. Stephens.

Old newspapers have proved a wonderful source of information about public houses. Such establishments often featured in minor court cases and so got a mention in the paper and that splendidly informative publication "The Sherborne Mercury" has been a valuable source for names and locations.

Some of the names of inns in bygone days would convey little now. The Cittern Inn which stood near the West Gate before the latter was demolished in the 1840s would have an unfamiliar ring today but when it was in existence in the 18th and 19th centuries it would have been quite an ordinary name to the citizens of Launceston, a cittern being a popular musical instrument resembling a lute which formed part of 'in-pub' entertainment in those days. Names which reflected well-known figures and/or processes in the woollen industry, then flourishing in Launceston, would also mean nothing to today's inhabitants.

The Ring o' Bells, still existing we are told, under the name of The Northgate Inn, referred in the 18th and 19th centuries to the craze for competition ringing of handbells. "The Sherborne Mercury" informs those with the patience to wade through its pages that a large silver bell was often the prize for competing teams, some of which travelled long distances to take part in the competitions.

Public houses were often the meeting places for the charitable organisations which were so much needed in those days when poverty was rife, and one of these was the long-defunct Launceston Charitable Society for the Benefit of Widows, Widowers, Orphans or Fatherless Children, which handed out small sums of money to the needy who came within its 'brief'. This particular organisation had its HQ at the Ring o' Bells and the landlord there was said to have actually instituted it.

The Bull's Head was reputed to be a popular haunt for farmers, whilst the Exeter Inn was favoured mainly by tradesmen, and there was also a Tradesmark Inn at one time. The Half Moon was situated outside the West Gate, where the Fire Station now stands, and got a lot of its trade from merchants approaching the town from that direction. The present Westgate Inn was originally called the New Gate in the days when the West Gate was still standing. Surely the West Gate was 'new' long before the existence of the public house, but perhaps it was the last of the three town gates to be built. It is not possible to establish that with certainty.

The Horse Dealers Inn spoke in its name for the nature of its clientele, but The Blacksmiths Arms was not so selective and catered for customers of all occupations it would seem. The location of The Castle Inn, mentioned in "The Sherborne Mercury", is unknown; The Cornubia is one to which there was fleeting reference in the Plymouth "Daily Mercury", and where was The Hunters Arms, mentioned in "The West Briton" in connection with a court case?

One of the oldest of the Launceston inns is reputed to be The Bell, beside St. Mary Magdelene Church, and which even today retains some of its original features. In the late 18th century it was greatly enlarged or what in today's parlance would be termed that cover-up for spoliation, 'developed'. The redoubtable "Sherborne Mercury" tells us that in March 1771 landlord William Ford put in hand plans for an extension of fourteen lodging rooms and stabling for fifty horses. Much later "The West Briton", another valuable source of early 19th century information, records that in 1847 the premises also included a slaughterhouse and covered skittle alley, and from the Bedford estates papers at the Devon County Record Office we glean that there was another Bell Inn in existence in 1757, being situated somewhere on the west side of the road from St. Stephens Church to St. Thomas Bridge, so presumably referring to St. Stephens Hill. At St. Stephens itself there were the Northumberland Arms (now a private dwelling known as Northumberland House) and The Valiant Soldier, both being parts of the then Duke of Northumberland's Werrington estate.

Even the vagrants had their own ale house, the Mumper's Inn, a mumper being defined in the dictionary as "one who begs in a whining tone"; in the case of Launceston, begging, presumably, to enable them to visit The Mumper's!

The really up-market establishment in the town was The White Hart, closely followed by The King's Arms. This writer's family had a special interest in the White Hart, a forebear at one time having a financial stake in it. It was in the late 18th century that the White Hart had its time of greatest elegance. Just prior to that the front entrance led into a central courtyard as was customary for such establishments in those days, but in 1762 one John Pearse became the owner and began to spruce things up. In 1762 he advertised that he had had the front of the building rebuilt and the interior entirely refurbished. There is speculation that this was the time when the Norman doorway, which almost certainly originated from the Priory, was installed. It made a most imposing entrance and still does so. Mr Pearse, the go getter of his day, also announced that public balls would be held in the new Long Room, which he claimed was the largest in Cornwall.

Despite all this, Mr Pearse's tenure of the establishment was not overlong. In 1774 Thomas Prockter was recorded as the owner and he too made improvements. By 1776 he was able to announce that his hotel offered three dining rooms and three parlours, up to sixty beds and stabling for sixty horses plus three post chaises with twelve horses - what more could the discerning traveller ask of a hostelry? After he died his widow remarried and remained what was described as 'hostess' at the White Hart until she died in 1816.

During the Assizes the Sheriff and his troop stayed at the White Hart and it is recorded that in 1794, when the Bishop of Exeter was in the town during a visitation and confirmation tour, he also stayed at the hotel and had special entertainment laid on for his benefit.

There is a curious little footnote to the history of the White Hart, to be found in a manuscript by one Thomas Tonkin and now in the possession of the library of the Royal Institution of Cornwall. Mr Tonkin writes that in 1731 he witnessed the performance of a raven kept at the hostelry and which obviously impressed him very much - "it spoke many words as plainly and distinctly as a parrot". Mr Tonkin goes on to say that the raven was kept in a pen in the courtyard but flew freely around the premises and that under the pen was a younger raven which was learning speech from its elder and which had already mastered several words! The landlord at the time bore the good Launceston name of Barriball, still borne by a number of residents of the town and surrounding area.

The White Hart in those days could also claim the distinction of having a theatre attached to it which attracted some quite notable performers. It was referred to as 'new' in the 1770s and in 1772 a great hit was The Exeter Company of Comedians who performed "Hamlet" there and, in complete contrast, a farce entitled "The Deuce is in Him", both of which apparently played to distinguished audiences.

Within living memory the White Hart retained some of its 18th century features. The foyer was unique; after entering the door the visitor was faced with the original 18th century bow-fronted window of the earlier building, then housing the office. All that has gone and the large recess which was the office forms part of the entrance lounge area with seating and small tables. The supposed site of the theatre and Assembly Rooms is now the White Hart shopping arcade, transformed in recent times from the hotel garage which superseded the theatre etc.

The Little White Hart was a much less prestigious establishment and stood on the site still known by older Launcestonians as Dunn's Corner at the junction of Western Road and The Square. There is a photograph of The Little White Hart among the archives of Lawrence House Museum in Launceston; it looks pretty dilapidated. Soon afterwards it was demolished and the "Launceston Weekly News" dated 21st December 1901 records that "On the site of the Little White Hart Hotel in Launceston, Mr W. V. Dunn has erected a handsome block of new premises". To this day that block of buildings is known as Dunn's Corner and if newcomers to the town may shake their heads in puzzlement when this well-known building is mentioned, we long-standing residents know better! Dunn's grocery store was a highly respected establishment, known almost county-wide, for a great many years until taken over by the Co-op after World War II. Since then the building has housed several different types of business and is at present occupied by a shop selling clothing, footwear and such.

The Dolphin stood on the site of the present fish and chip restaurant in Westgate Street and was regarded as a hostelry frequented by skilled tradesmen such as master carpenters.

In the archives of Werrington Park a book entitled "A Survey of the Manor of Launceston Land", actually an inventory of land owned by the compiler, the Rt. Hon. Humphry Morice in 1770, mention is made of one John Hawkins, occupier of the Rose and Crown Inn in High Street and William Symons, occupier of "The Little White Hart adjoining", so that is another hostelry the

The White Hart Hotel decorated for a Royal Visit by the Duke and Duchess of Cornwall (later George V and Queen Mary) in 1909, when the Duke received the Feudal Dues.

The famous Norman Doorway at the White Hart Hotel. Also visible is the bow-fronted window of the earlier building, then incorporated into the foyer.

The Kings Arms Hotel decorated for the same Royal Visit.

RIP ROARING LAUNCESTON!

location of which can be pinpointed.

We have headed this chapter "Rip Roaring Launceston" and with so many public houses and ale houses in the town, plus a proliferation of pretty rumbustious residents, it was not uncommon for disturbances to occur. We tend to think of violence on the streets as a product of modern times but even if a hundred years ago guns and knives were not freely carried - and used, fisticuffs could inflict quite an appreciable amount of damage. For instance, in the "Launceston Weekly News" of 19th December 1891 we read that "A serious row occurred in Broad Street, Launceston, on Saturday evening, when Constable Well was severely mauled by several young men and had to be escorted away under protection". His job could not have been an easy one: in 1870 the police force in the town consisted of just one constable, and that in a town with nearly three thousand inhabitants.

The Castle Temperance Hotel in High Street. There are now modern shops on the site.

The Castle Hotel Bus which used to meet guests at the railway station and take them back there at the end of their stay.

CHAPTER 6
Gaols and Punishment

Launceston's history as far as gaols are concerned is a pretty grim one and still intact are some reminders of the days when humane treatment of prisoners was not considered necessary or even desirable.

The Southgate looks pleasant enough today but up until 1884 it was known as The Dark House and not without reason. It is recorded that as far back as 1381 two keepers were employed to guard prisoners in the South Gate of the town walls. From an old document in the town archives we learn that '1567 - Robert Craghte and Hatie doth occupy. Kept for common use of town'. In 1805 it was described as 'a most filthy and dilapidated place'. A keeper at that time made frequent applications to the mayor of Launceston for whitewash to lighten up the place but he always had the same reply - "The blacker it is the better, it has more appearance of a jail that way". In some rooms the doors were only four feet high and fifteen inches wide. The upper room was the debtors' prison and the lower room was for petty offenders. The only light came from an aperture three feet by nine inches and that was almost obscured by iron bars. Straw was scattered on the floor. There was a fireplace but no fuel was allowed. A bath tub also served as a toilet. There was no courtyard and no water. Could any worse conditions possibly be imagined? Overcrowding was also the order of the day: the lower room was intended to house twenty-five petty offenders at any one time and in 1827 five burglars were sleeping in one bed, which caused some caring people to send a report to the Home Secretary, requesting that he intervene in the running of the gaol. The Southgate finally ceased being used as a prison as late of 1884 and in 1886 The Launceston Historical and Scientific Society converted it into a museum. The heavy old door of the Southgate is said to have originally been the entrance door to the condemned cell of the old prison in what are now the Castle grounds. It still serves today as the entrance door to the Southgate.

If conditions were bad in the Southgate in the 19th century they were certainly not much better in the County Gaol which was built within the Castle bailey.

The official report of the conditions in the prison gives a true picture of what it was really like. In 1775 in his report on States of the Prisons - Western Circuit (Cornwall) John Howard wrote:-

"This gaol, though built in a large yard belonging to the old ruinous Castle, is very small; house and court measuring only fifty two feet by forty four; and the house not covering half that ground. The Prison is a room or passage twenty three feet and a half by seven and a half, with only one window two feet by one and a half - and three Dungeons or Cages on the side opposite the window: these are about six and half feet deep; one nine feet long; one about eight; one not five: this last for women. They are all very offensive. No chimney: no drains: no water: damp earth floors: no Infirmary. The yard not secure; and Prisoners seldom permitted to go out to it. Indeed the whole Prison is out of repair. and yet the Gaoler lives distant. I once found the Prisoners chained two or three together. Their provision is put down to them through a hole (nine inches by eight) in the floor of the room above (used as a Chapel); and those who serve them there, often catch the fatal fever. At my first visit I found the Keeper, his Assistant, and all the Prisoners but one, sick of it; and heard that a few years before, many Prisoners had died of it; and the Keeper and his wife in one night.

"I learned that a woman who was discharged just before my first visit (by the Grand Jury making a collection for her Fees) had been confined three years by the Ecclesiastical Court; and had three

GAOLS AND PUNISHMENT

The South Gate, or Southgate as it is known today, in the late 1920s or early '30s (above), and in the late '30s or early '40s. The sycamore tree which grew out of the masonry was famous and there was great sadness in the town when it was removed in recent times because it was claimed to be damaging the structure.

GAOLS AND PUNISHMENT

children in the Gaol. There is no Table of Fees.

"The King, of his Royal Bounty, has offered TWO THOUSAND POUNDS towards a new Gaol; but nothing is done by the County.

"I was edified by the serious behaviour of the Chaplain at Prayers. The Prisoners respect him, and were very attentive. He has a large family: I was sorry for the late reduction of his Salary.

"The Mayor sends the Prisoners weekly one shilling's worth of bread; no memorial of the legacy in the Gaol. Transports have not the King's allowance of 2s 6d a week. Clauses of Act against Spirituous Liquors not hung up".

Before its closure things had perhaps improved slightly. In 1892 a Mr Langman, a builder in Launceston, who well remembered the old County Gaol, wrote an account of his reminiscences in a diary and he paints a quite vivid picture of what the buildings and some of the conditions were like.

The gaol was demolished in 1842 and the only reminder of it today is the pump which still stands in what are now the Castle grounds. The pump was the water supply for the gaol and it bears the date 1778. It was presumably installed as a result of John Howard's damning report of 1775. At one time the prisoners petitioned to keep poultry but it was not allowed because it was deemed the birds would disturb the priest.

Pump which served the County Gaol, in situ in the Castle grounds which were formerly the gaol courtyard.

But to get back to Mr Langman's memories. He recorded that on the ground floor there was a range of five cells, nine feet by eight feet, also a kitchen which was twenty feet square and situated in the left wing on the southern side. The courtyard was about thirty feet wide and the length of the kitchen and the cells and was about four feet from the entrance to the yard. From Castle Dyke to the gaol the direction was north east. The entrance which led from the governor's apartments was about nine feet wide and over a stone staircase of sixteen steps, where the bell rope was fixed to time meals and the prisoners' time to go to rest. On the left hand side were the men's cells but the condemned cells (four in all) were on the right hand side, beneath the women's apartments. Large rings were fixed in the floor for the purpose of chaining criminals. In the females' apartment above there were also four cells. The women's yard was about forty feet by twenty feet; they were, of course, segregated from the men. At the time of a gaol delivery there were frequently four or five prisoners in a cell and if the prison was 'overcrowded' then the Dark House was cleared for the accommodation of prisoners.

John Mules was governor of the County Gaol until his death in 1803, when he was succeeded by his son Christopher Mules, who held the post until the abolition in 1830 of the gaol as a place of detention, when he was transferred to Bodmin Gaol as a warder.

Immediately after the demolition of the gaol building a wall was built surrounding the castle grounds. Christopher Mules's widow held possession until the demolition.

In the time of John Mules, prisoners were taken to St. Mary's Church for spiritual consolation.

The other walls of the gaol were about twenty-two feet high. An old door, recorded as standing in 1892 on the late Mr Ching's property at Hendra, Western Road, formerly belonged to the gaol and was the door which led from the females' ward and through which had to pass all criminals who were tried at the Assizes. (Whether or not this was the door which is now the entrance to the Southgate is not known). "Until 1892," continues Mr Langman, "there was another of the old gaol doors at Werrington Park but in 1892 that one was demolished." These days such relics would be carefully preserved but in the 19th century, although regarded as macabre novelties at the time, their appeal soon faded and they were thrown out.

There was an entrance to the County Gaol from Castle Dyke at the back of the then Wesleyan Chapel, commonly called Stingnettle Lane. Over

GAOLS AND PUNISHMENT

Dungeons at Bridewell.

the entrance to the gaol was a sign board which proclaimed "No admittance except by an Order from the Sheriff or a Magistrate".

It is interesting and very enlightening to read the details for the "County Gaol at Launceston, For Felons" as recorded by John Howard in 1780. These read as follows:-
GAOLER, John Mules, deputy, under Coryndon Carpenter Esq, constable of the castle (since dead). Salary, lately augmented by the county from £8 to £12.
Fees, Felons, £0:16:8.
Transports, 4d a mile each.
Licence, none.
PRISONERS,
Allowance, Felons, a three-penny loaf each in two days; white or brown at their option (weight in Dec. 1775, of white bread 1lb 10oz; brown, 2lb 2oz.
Number,

Felons etc.		Felons etc.	
1774, Feb. 19	11	1775, Dec. 23	6
____, Sep. 13	8	1779, Feb. 4	4

CHAPLAIN, Rev. Mr. Lethbridge.
Duty, Tuesday and Friday.
Salary, £50.
SURGEON, Mr. Bennet.
Salary, £15.

In his 1780 report Mr Howard augmented his 1775 report by concluding "Neither clauses against spirituous liquors, nor the act for preserving the health of prisoners, are hung up". His earlier report had not mentioned the health of prisoners. There was also information about some slight improvements to the gaol - "The king, of his royal bounty, offered £2500 towards a new gaol; but nothing had been done in the county by 1776. Now, in 1779, there is a new gaol for men-felons, consisting of four cells (8 feet by 6½, and 8 feet high) a day-room and a court. Over the rooms are the gaoler's apartments. Adjoining is the old gaol, which is to be repaired for women-felons, as £500 of the king's bounty is appropriated to that purpose."

Another of Launceston's notorious gaols was the Bridewell. It was set on land which sloped away to the Kensey valley and its remains are at the back of the old workhouses (now terrace cottages) in Dockacre Road (then known as Horse Lane). It is believed to have been built on the site of Sibard Wells about 1466 or earlier.

The first mention of the Bridewell gaol came in 1663, when it was reported in London that seven Quakers had been apprehended in Somerset and sent to Lanson (sic) Jail on 9th November 1663. Among them was a young man of nineteen, Josiah Coale (or Coates) who produced a violently worded pamphlet directed against the Church of Rome and which he signed as having been "Written in Bridewel, near Lanston. in Cornwall. the 11th Moneth. 1664". In its later years the Bridewell was used for "the punishment of disobedient and unmanageable paupers". It had no water supply and no sanitation and was described as 'very dirty' by prison reformer James Neild after he visited it in 1806. The prison was closed down some time between 1836 and 1839. But reminders of its horrors still remain. There are still intact two cells, each with its original granite lintel. These are now used for storage purposes but in the walls are still the thick iron rings used for the chaining of prisoners. What grim stories they could tell. It is still a sobering experience to touch them and let the imagination do the rest. There were riots in the Bridewell in 1836 when families were separated for some to be accommodated in the new workhouse at Pages Cross.

In 1834 a young man was tied to a tree which stood in the centre of the old workhouse yard and given 25 lashes prior to 3 months imprisonment in Bridewell for assault, but within a few years Bridewell, the Law Courts in Broad Street, and flogging were all things of the past.

Considerable alterations have been made to the former workhouse and Bridewell site in recent years. Buildings have been transformed into luxury flats and the site partially landscaped. But still, hidden among undergrowth on the sloping land which runs towards the Kensey valley, odd stones and bits of foundations of the old Bridewell may be located. And one mystery concerning the former workhouse buildings has never been solved. In the book "Gateway to Cornwall", published in 1981, this writer drew attention to two bricks in the wall above a window and with scratched upon them "I. Beard 1754". To this date the mystery of who I. Beard might have been has never been solved. The 'I' was actually the old way of writing the capital letter 'J', so who was J. Beard and why did he have his name and date in such a prominent place in a public building? Was he the first ever Master of the new workhouse, such a person being allowed the honour of scratching his name or initials on one of the bricks in a prominent position? But the workhouse was not actually built until 1760: in fact, it was not until 1755 that a Petition was presented to the House of Commons for the building of the workhouse. In 1754 there was a Local Act of Parliament under which Guardians of the Poor were invested in the Town Council, so was Mr Beard perhaps the chairman of the Guardians at that time? No mention of him ever appears to have been recorded. Fortunately when the building was converted a few years ago the inscribed stone was left intact, so it is still there for all to see and speculate about.

CHAPTER 7
Launceston as a Parole Town

There is one period of Launceston's history about which not much has been written, yet it had a profound effect on the town and its inhabitants.

The Napoleonic Wars raged from 1793 to 1815 and during that period a prodigious number of prisoners-of-war were taken; it was estimated that over 60,000 were housed in England, in prisons, or prison ships, or later in private houses.

In the south west, Dartmoor Prison was built specially to house them but even that huge building proved inadequate and the idea of the parole town was established. Prisoners-of-war were billeted on private families. It was not a new concept: Launceston had been a parole town during the Seven Years War from 1756-63; the difference was that the French P.O.W. operation was more organised and the numbers to be accommodated were far greater. So Launceston 'did its bit' in this respect from 1803 to 1813.

The men were quartered in private houses on condition that they gave their word of honour not to attempt to escape. If that seems pretty naive, even laughable, today, it must be remembered that in years past a word of honour was a serious undertaking and most especially among the French, who even to this day regard it as something mildly sacred. The prisoners were treated fairly liberally: each received a fixed sum (half a guinea, 52½p today) per week for maintenance and the householder taking them in also received the same sum for each man. The men were allowed to engage in any kind of business or occupation (provided it was legal) to augment their incomes and they were also allowed to use any private funds which they may have had available, or which might have been sent to them by their relatives in France. They were overseen by a government agent, in the case of Launceston one Mr Spettigue, who lived in the house in Castle Street now known as Trevean.

Agent Spettigue was responsible for doling out the maintenance and lodging money and for ensuring the prisoners obeyed the curfew rules. The men had to be in their lodgings by 5pm in winter and 8pm in summer but there is evidence that this rule was not strictly kept, especially as time wore on and familiarity bred contempt.

The majority of the prisoners quartered in Launceston were naval officers and both they and the lesser ranks among them had a variety of skills which proved invaluable in the town. Several of the officers augmented their income by teaching French, others even coached the illiterate members of the community in the rudiments of reading and writing English! Education became a two-way traffic in one case. The Rev'd Thomas Byrth, born in Plymouth in 1799, later to become a clergyman and highly regarded as an intellectual, was sent to Launceston at the age of fifteen to attend Dr Cope's Academy, a well-known seminary housed first at Belle Vue and later at Eagle House. There the young Thomas Byrth studied Hebrew and French and he was reported to have made great progress in the latter language by practising it on the prisoners-of-war in the town.

Another way in which the Frenchmen helped the population of Launceston was as doctors, advising on the use of simple medicine, whilst others are reputed to have worked wonders as herbalists, treating a large proportion of the population with herbal remedies which they made up from plants which they gathered locally.

Castle Street was at that time the top residential area of the town; with its large houses it was far more suitable for housing extra 'visitors' than the tiny cottages and hovels in the cramped town centre, so it was in the Castle Street area that the majority of the prisoners were quartered.

Mr Smith-Pearse, a dedicated Methodist and

member of a well-known old Launceston family, had several prisoners living at his house in Castle Street in 1810. He was horrified when by chance he came upon a bill for beer which one of his 'guests' received, and is recorded as saying that "they drank freely and appreciated drink". In Launceston Museum are the covers which are all that remain of the "French Gentlemen's Beer Account 1812", the words written on the front cover. The prisoners often played dominoes with Mr Smith-Pearse's elderly father and they gave him a small shoe of carved wood containing a tiny set of bone dominoes. It has been handed down in the family but its present whereabouts are unknown.

To digress here - many of the prisoners were skilled craftsmen who had been employed in the ivory carving industry in Dijon and they used the bones from their meat ration to make models which ranged from fully rigged sailing ships to 'automated' guillotines and miniature boxes of dominoes or gaming counters. I am personally the owner of a minute box of perfectly made dominoes which was given to my late mother when she was a very small child by a friend of my grandparents whom she knew as 'Grandpa' Gruzelier.

It has now been established that Mr Gruzelier was a French prisoner of war in Launceston; he stayed on after the war and married a local girl who was a friend of my grandparents. He founded a dynasty which still exists: there are several Gruzeliers buried in the old cemetery in Dockacre Road. My grandparents and members of the

Miniature box of dominoes made from meat bones by a Napoleonic POW in Launceston. Compared to a 2p coin.

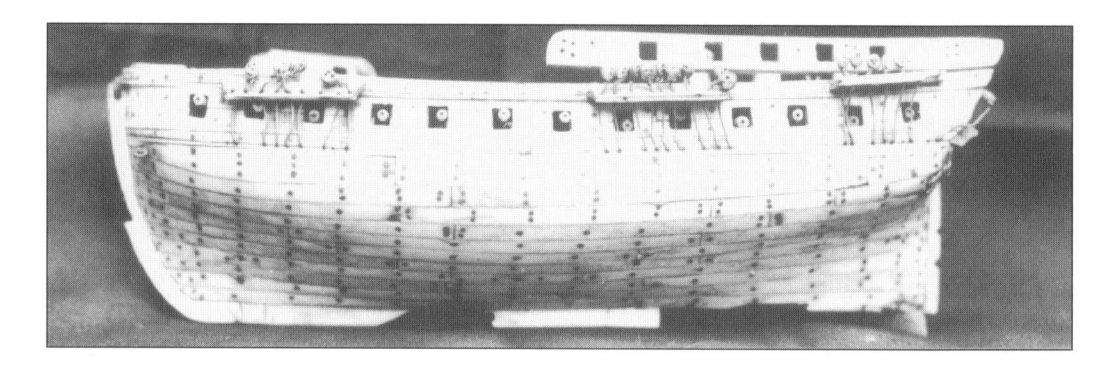

Model ship made by Napoleonic Prisoners of War in Launceston. Now in the Lawrence House Museum.

Gruzelier family later moved to west Cornwall and there are today four people of that name listed in the telephone directory, two of them in Penzance, one in Newlyn and one in Mousehole. There are also Gruzeliers buried in Paul churchyard. My mother was born in Helston and lived there as a child with her parents.

So, to get back to the prisoners in Launceston and their effect on the town. Quite a number of the prisoners married local girls in the towns in which they were quartered although this practice was discouraged by the authorities. In Launceston there are no references in the St. Thomas and St. Stephen church registers but at St. Mary Magdalene between 2nd July 1757 and 20th April 1809 twelve burials are recorded and the names include one Spanish prisoner called Joseph Garcia, buried on 21st January 1808. Between 18th November 1807 and 5th August 1817 eleven marriages are recorded, five by banns and six by licence.

In 1844 one of the prisoners' benefactors, Mr William Pearse, died and in its issue of October 1844 "The Wesleyan Methodist Magazine" published a memoir of him in which it lavishly paid tribute to his work with the prisoners, saying "Mr Pearse deeply sympathised with these unhappy captives and sought their highest good. He procured tracts in their different languages and gave them religious instruction. He also relieved the necessities of those who were in distress. Many of these gentlemen professed to be very thankful for these attentions and some attended regularly the public worship of Almighty God".

Mr Pearse probably converted some of the prisoners to the Wesleyan doctrine although it could not have been an easy task. The older men among the prisoners were mainly Roman Catholic but some of the younger and more 'modern' ones were disciples of Voltaire and it is doubtless among them that Mr Pearse concentrated his greatest energies in preaching Methodism.

One of the prisoners returned to his homeland at the General Peace but had married a local girl and he came back to Launceston and was employed by the trustees of the Wesleyan Chapel in the town as a caretaker. When he died he was buried in the Wesleyan graveyard at the bottom of St. Thomas Hill.

Now in July 1990 there is an interesting possible sequel to that story. Renovation was taking place at the present Central Methodist Chapel in the town and plaster was stripped away from a wall surrounding a window half way up the staircase leading to the balcony. This revealed that when that particular extension was made to the chapel the stone used had come from an older, demolished, building. One of the stones is a fairly thick slate, obviously used as a facing stone, and on it is scratched some wording. The inscription was done with some sharp instrument such as a nail and is almost indecipherable but careful scrutiny appears to reveal the first word 'Qui', followed by 'pl' and 'expat ...'. The wording could be French and it could have been scratched by that French prisoner

Inscribed stone in the wall of the Central Methodist Chapel.

who lived in the cottage attached to the chapel and which was demolished to provide materials for the construction of an extension to the building which is now known as Central Methodist Chapel. Consider the possibilities - 'Qui' = which; 'pleurs' = tears; s'expatrier - leave one's country. Could that have been a somewhat poignant statement scratched on a stone in the front of his cottage by the former French prisoner-of-war who later became caretaker of the Wesleyan chapel?

Of course, not all the French prisoners were pious models of society. The Frenchmen must have seemed very racy to many members of the population in Launceston and the local boys soon picked up the word 'morbleu' which they heard the Frenchmen use frequently, the English equivalent of which is defined in the dictionary as 'zounds! An obsolete oath, an exclamation of anger etc.' There were a few clever forgers among the prisoners and The Launceston and Totnes Bank was one of their favourite victims. A representative of this bank used to attend the regular markets held outside Dartmoor Prison at which the prisoners sold the items they had made - bone models, inlaid straw work, trinkets made from human hair, and so on. The bank was so greatly defrauded that its representative was instructed to write his name on all notes offered by prisoners for goods received. "The Plymouth & Dock Telegraph", a popular newspaper of the period, reported that in 1812 one Pierre de Romfort (alias Pierre de la Roche) a prisoner-of-war on parole at Launceston, was hanged at Bodmin for forgery and it says "He behaved very penitently and was attended to at the last moment by Mr Lefers, a Roman Catholic priest living at Lanherne".

There was also an element of unscrupulous people in Launceston who did everything they could to encourage the prisoners to break their parole. This was mainly because a reward of ten shillings could be claimed by anyone who reported and caused to be a caught a prisoner breaking parole, or sixpence for anyone tipping off agent Spettigue of such an incident which did not result in recapture. Agent Spettigue also employed a small number of "undercover agents" to assist him and the notebook of one of these people, now in the possession of a member of a prominent Cornish family, includes the entries "For watching the Frenchmen ... 1/-"; "Beer for the Frenchmen ... 1/-"; "Meat and drink for the Frenchmen ... 3/-".

The boundary line for French officers on parole in Launceston was one mile from the town centre. Granite stones with "1 mile" carved into them marked the boundary and the one at Polson Bridge remained within living memory until removed and lost forever during roadworks in the area. Anyone found beyond the boundary faced the punishment of forfeiting his parole and being sent back to Dartmoor Prison. In Launceston Museum is a copy of a painting entitled "Vue de Launceston" taken from an original by a French prisoner and it has a story behind it. One Dr Pethick was a pupil as a boy at a local grammar school when one summer Saturday afternoon in 1808 he was bathing in Kensey Pool, just above the then headweir below

Picture painted by a Napoleonic POW in Launceston. Now in the Lawrence House Museum.

what was then called East Ridgegrove Lane. He ventured into deep water, got into difficulties and was rescued by two French officers who happened to be passing and heard his cries for help. Although by going to his help they were breaking parole by being just outside the one mile boundary, they helped the boy out and his parents were eternally grateful and became very friendly with the two officers, engaging them to teach the other Pethick children the French language. The boy who later was 'Dr' Pethick, became so fond of the two men that he visited them almost every year after they returned to France. He bought the original of the "Vue de Launceston" direct from one of them who had painted it.

There were also other hazards facing the prisoners, not always of their own making. "The Plymouth and Dock Telegraph" dated 16th November 1811 carried a report which informs us that "On Tuesday last an officers' guard belonging to the Somerset Militia proceeded to Lanson for the purpose of escorting all the French prisoners of the rank of Midshipman on parole at that place to the prison at Dartmoor. The number of prisoners so sent amounted to 37. Their removal has been occasioned by the French Government to imprison all Midshipmen amongst the British P.O.W. in France".

The newspapers of the time carried many advertisements for information concerning prisoners who had broken parole. "The Western Flying Post" of Launceston, dated 1756, offered two guineas reward for the recapture of two who had broken parole, in the following terms: "One M. Barbier, a short man, somewhat pock-marked and has a very dejected look and wore a snuff coloured coat. The other, M. Beth, a middle-aged man, very strongly set, wore his own hair and a blue coat. The former speaks no English, but the latter very well. They were both last seen near Exeter, riding to that city". Then a news item in "The Royal Cornwall Gazette" dated 25th November 1809 reads "Five French officers who broke their parole of honour and escaped last week from Lanson, were all taken near Looe and are confined on board the prison ship at Plymouth".

A little-known feature of the life of the French prisoners in Launceston is their involvement in Freemasonry. Several joined the Dunheved Lodge of Freemasons and records show that the Lodge was in existence at the time of the Seven Years War. Among those records is the information that in 1757 a Capt. N. de Court sent a letter to the Grand Lodge asking if it could provide his liberty to return to Bordeaux. That could not be met but he was granted the sum of twenty pounds relief.

Officers who joined the Dunheved Lodge are recorded as:

Turquoise Chevalier de Quance joined 4.4.1758
Christopher Craville (Surgeon) joined 4.12.1761
François Louis Baptiste, 8.8.1826. (Listed as "A Rogue". What *did* he do?!)
Chevalier de la Peré, Commander of the 'Mignone'.

A French Prisoner-of-War Lodge - Consolante Maconne - existed in Launceston during five of the years of the Seven Years War but the only documentary evidence concerning it is to be found in two certificates issued in 1762 and 1763. The former is in French and issued by a Frenchman, the other in English and issued to Mr Robert Martin, organist at St. Mary Magdalene Church, who was buried in the churchyard there in 1800. As far as can be proved this was the only French Prisoner-of-War Lodge that ever existed in Cornwall. Incidentally, the two certificates both have French signatories - five on the 1762 one and four on the 1763 one.

It is known that the French prisoners at Launceston made handsome Masonic apparel and jewels. Brother Mons Galopin made wonderful aprons etc. and an apron and a sash which he made were exhibited by Worshipful Brother R. Pearce Couch at Falmouth many years ago and were afterwards given to the Quatuor Coronati Lodge.

This chapter must end with one of the most extraordinary stories ever told about French prisoners of war in England. It happens to relate to one of the Frenchmen quartered in Launceston and is put together from a series of letters now in the Public Records Office in London.

Louis Vanhille was purser of the privateer "Pandour" and was sent to Launceston on parole on 12th May 1806. Then aged thirty two years, he was said to be "small in stature, agreeable of face although pock-marked, fair, as befitted his Flemish origin, and spoke almost perfect English". He was also financially stable: "Pandour" was a successful privateer and he received a great deal of prize money. He was also a great charmer and ladies' man.

In Launceston, Vanhille found himself billeted with the family of one John Tyeth, a brewer and a pious Baptist. Mr Tyeth and his wife had three married daughters and two unmarried ones, and the two unmarried ones, Fanny and her sister, kept the Post Office at Launceston. One of Mr Tyeth's daughters was married to the Rev'd Bunsell, vicar of Launceston, and was considered pretty high on the social ladder in the town.

Vanhille soon weighed up the situation and saw it offered considerable advantages to him. He soon became a Baptist convert and paid particular attention to the reputedly plain-looking Fanny, who was useful to him because of her Post Office connections. John Tyeth was not at all happy with the situation because in common with most English people of the time he looked upon all Frenchmen as atheists and revolutionaries. In the case of Vanhille he was probably not far off the mark!

His charm and courtly manners won Vanhille friends and his social life flourished inasmuch as was possible for a prisoner. A spinster and straw hat maker, a Miss Johanna Colwell, lived opposite the brewery and took pity on Vanhille, doing all she could to make him feel at home in a strange country. Further along the street was billeted Vanhille's best friend, a Dr Derouge, an army surgeon, who was placed with a Mr Pearson and his family. Vanhille owed a special debt of gratitude to Derouge, because the latter had cured him of smallpox. Vanhille also became acquainted and later very friendly with a Dr Mabyn of Camelford and in Launceston he was welcomed into the homes of Mr Dale, an ironmonger, and Mr John Rowe, a tailor, both comparatively well-to-do and highly respected residents of the town.

Vanhille appears to have had an extraordinary amount of freedom. One wonders what agent Spettigue was about, obviously not carrying out his duties very conscientiously in the case of Louis Vanhille; possible he also had come under the spell of the charismatic character. Vanhille totally ignored the one mile boundary limit: he went to Camelford to dine with Dr Mabyn and he rode to Tavistock on the Tyeth family's pony, ostensibly to visit the Pearce family, ironmongers of high repute, but actually on a romantic mission to see the Misses Annie and Elizabeth Penwarden, who were described at the time as "gay young milliners" and who both spoke French. Vanhille was also seen frequently in the company of Fanny Tyeth, who took him to visit her aunt in Tavistock and he was generally regarded as Fanny's fiancé, although he took great care to ensure that was not 'official'.

Meanwhile Derouge, "a man of sombre countenance", did not enjoy nearly as much popularity and found captivity extremely irksome, so Vanhille, taking advantage of this, worked out a plot. Derouge's lack of popularity was said to be largely due the fact that he got a local girl pregnant and the higher echelons of Launceston society were scandalised and ostracised him.

When the child was born the mother could not afford to look after it and it fell to the authorities to pay for its subsistence. Mr Proctor, the Guardian of the Poor for the town, and agent Spettigue ordered Derouge to pay £25 towards the child's upkeep. This he apparently could not do, but Vanhille, with an ulterior motive, paid it for him.

What happened then is not clear, there are some vital gaps, but in a letter to the Admiralty, dated 5th December 1811, we learn that Vanhille and Derouge had tried to escape but were betrayed by a member of the Portuguese Army (how he came to be in Launceston is not recorded) and they were foiled in their plan and as a punishment sent to Dartmoor Prison on 12th December 1811. Mr Spettigue was ordered by the Transport Office to keep a close watch on the Tyeth family and Vanhille's other friends, all of whom were suspected of aiding and abetting him.

Somewhat surprisingly the good citizens of Launceston took strong exception to this, so well had the two prisoners ingratiated themselves with the town's merchants and professional people, and these locally influential people even got their Member of Parliament, a Mr Giddy, to intercede with the Transport Office and request the reinstatement of the two men on parole, but this request was turned down.

Vanhille soon tired of prison life and at the daily market which was held at the prison gates, when prisoners sold their craftwork and bought food and clothes from local people, Vanhille 'chatted up' one Mary Ellis. She, like all the other women, fell under his spell and daily brought him from Tavistock items for a disguise - an old broad-brimmed hat, a dark coat, heavy boots and brown stockings. On 22nd August 1812 Vanhille made his bid for freedom, donning all the clothing he had acquired from Mary Ellis, and with her connivance mingled with the market traders, eventually getting on to the main road. He walked to Tavistock and by methods unknown got back to Launceston that same night and was eagerly taken in by the Tyeths.

However, his stay in the town was short. The following day he went (again by what means is not recorded) to Camelford and called on Dr Mabyn. Then he moved on to Padstow and tried to get a boatman to take him to Bristol or Cork, but he could not persuade any boatman to take him and so he returned to Launceston, frustrated but not beaten. On that occasion he stayed in Launceston two days, during which time he succeeded in buying a map (another commodity forbidden to prisoners), changed his disguise and assumed that of one Williams, a pedlar.

In his new disguise he got as far as Bideford and

LAUNCESTON AS A PAROLE TOWN

No. 9 Castle Street, formerly the HQ of Napoleonic POWs in Launceston. Now the Lawrence House Museum.

that proving not suitable for his purpose he moved on to Appledore. There he was more successful and secured a passage in a boat to Newport, from where he travelled to another crowded parole town, Abergavenny, where he renewed acquaintance with a prisoner called Palierne, who had been with him in Launceston. For some reason unknown and rather riskily one would have thought, Vanhille went back to Launceston and stayed there for two days after which his exploits became even more bizarre. He went back to Abergavenny, via Okehampton, Exeter, Taunton, London and Chatham and then down the river Usk to Bristol, where he hoped to be able to get a ship to spirit him to America. This bid was unsuccessful so back he went to Launceston by coach and stayed two weeks with the Tyeths, who were still so much under his spell that they readily accommodated him. All this was going on under the nose of agent Spettigue who must have been purposely blind or extremely stupid. One can only assume that there must have been some financial consideration involved.

At the end of two weeks Vanhille moved to Falmouth and then to Bristol again. All the time he corresponded with his Launceston friends and the highly respectable Tyeths even replied to him, disguising their writing and signature, and Miss Fanny Tyeth at the Post Office would even painstakingly obliterate the postmark. Old Mr Tyeth is even said to have sent Vanhille "kind and pious messages". It was an incredible state of affairs which even today makes the mind boggle.

Vanhille finally succeeded in getting from Bristol to Jamaica but there the authorities were obviously more vigilant and he was caught and returned to England, where he was forced to submit to cross-questioning by a Mr Jones of Knight & Jones, solicitors to the Admiralty, with the object of getting from Vanhille information concerning his friends and accomplices in Launceston, as the town had gained a notorious reputation for its sympathy with the prisoners. To his credit, Vanhille refused to incriminate anyone. Sadly, his erstwhile friends were not so loyal. Mr Dale, the once prosperous ironmonger, had "fallen into evil ways" and was discovered to be starving in Plymouth. He sent a letter to Mr Jones saying that he was willing to denounce all Vanhille's friends in Launceston - for a consideration. Whether or not his offer was taken up is not recorded.

Dr Derouge was taken from Dartmoor to London and under pressure he revealed all the names of Vanhille's associates in Launceston. They were all summoned but amazingly none of them would give any information. A Mrs Wilkins, an innkeeper who had fallen foul of Vanhille, pressed anxiously to give evidence but when questioned it was found that she had none of consequence to give! Ironmonger Dale, meanwhile, had some success in his bid for recognition and was sent to Launceston at government expense to try to get more information, but he too failed.

LAUNCESTON AS A PAROLE TOWN

The outcome of all this is that Vanhille was the winner in the end because the Peace of 1814 meant that he was released and he immediately returned to France, arriving at Calais on 19th April 1814.

So ends probably one of the most extraordinary stories ever to emerge from the town of Launceston. What happened to the Tyeths, who were so scandalously involved in the plot, is not known: there is no record of their fate. In all, the astonishing Vanhille spent fifty five days travelling by foot, carriage and boat and covered one thousand two hundred and thirty eight miles, and if you doubt any of that, it can all be seen written in black and white.

Incidentally, there is in St. Mary's Church one relic of those hectic days, although not connected in any way with Vanhille. It is a crucifix said to have been looted by a Frenchman from a church in Spain during the Peninsular War. The man later came to Launceston as a French prisoner on parole and stayed with Mr Abraham Shepheard in Broad Street. Mr Shepheard was a hat maker, hat making being at that time one of the most important industries in the town. When the prisoner left Launceston at the Peace in 1814 he gave the crucifix to one of Mr Shepheard's family and it was handed down in the family until it got to Abraham's granddaughter, who married her cousin Thomas Shearme Jnr. Through this union the crucifix came into the possession of their son John Shearme of Looe, who gave it to St. Mary's Church to be placed in the Lady Chapel.

Eagle House, built by Coryndon Carpenter in the 18th century. The decorative plaster ceilings and a frieze in the former dining room are said to have been done by Napoleonic POWs.

CHAPTER 8
The Second Military Invasion

If the French prisoners revolutionised life in Launceston in the early 19th century, equally radical reforms (or should it be mayhem?!) occurred over a century later when the Americans hit town.

One day they weren't there, the next day the town was filled with them. In late 1942 American troops had been arriving in Britain and were being scattered in camps throughout the country. At first no one ever thought they would be in Launceston, then rumours began to spread - the Americans were coming to Launceston. No, it couldn't be true, said the older folk; we certainly hope it is, murmured the young women!

Of course they did come, a section of the huge 29th Infantry Division which was spread over the south west and which distinguished itself so splendidly on D-Day with the landing on Omaha Beach. They were white troops and they were supported by the coloured troops of the Ordnance Battalions.

Probably the biggest novelty was the appearance of coloured troops. Many people, especially in the more remote country districts, had never before seen a black man in the flesh and the 'boys' immediately got christened 'the darkies', a title which they accepted with good humour and not a little amusement. They were kind hearted and helpful in many ways. They would often lift little old ladies bodily into their large trucks to provide a (strictly speaking, illegal) lift into town from the outlying districts when shortage and rationing of fuel meant car journeys could only be made for seriously essential purposes and bus services were almost non existent. They distributed Hershey candy bars ad lib. Hershey bars were highly favoured by the Americans; the sweetmeat was a sort of nut toffee which all the locals found stuck around their teeth and was not particularly to their taste but all recipients savoured it with great gusto because (a) it was American and therefore it must be good, (b) it was a novelty and sweet tooths in a candy starved Britain were prepared to enjoy anything to satisfy their craving, and (c) it was free! Oranges and cigarettes were also handed out to all and sundry without looking for any reward. Some young children had never before seen an orange: for two years they had been off the market in Britain; smokers were not wildly enthusiastic about Camels or Lucky Strike (the most popular American cigarette brands) but soon got into the way of opening one corner of the soft packet and tipping a cigarette directly between their lips, American fashion.

The white soldiers were more prone to distributing Du Pont nylon stockings, the greatest dream of every young girl at the time. They were a much thicker denier than the gossamer knits available today but were such a wonderful luxury improvement on coating bare legs in a sort of suntan lotion and running a dark eyebrow pencil up the back to simulate a seam. Seamless stockings were *not* 'the thing' in those days.

Needless to say, the public houses in town had a field day or rather, days. The Americans favoured spirits and Bourbon on the Rocks was a frequent order. There was no official segregation of 'white' or 'black' public houses although the two sections did tend to congregate separately in different hostelries. No establishments were officially off limits: the men operated their own segregation arrangements. This all seemed to work fairly smoothly until one early evening on a September Sunday in 1943 when Launceston was turned for a brief period into a Wild West frontier town or Chicago's gangland - if you can imagine that!

Here personal reminiscences must come into the story because I have vivid memories of being

THE SECOND MILITARY INVASION

almost in the line of fire on that momentous occasion. The trouble started when white soldiers 'invaded' a bar where black soldiers were drinking. Legend has it that it was The White Hart, although some claim it was The King's Arms; that will probably always remain a bone of contention. Tempers flared when the white troops allegedly provoked the blacks and (although forbidden to be carried) guns were drawn. A running battle ensued and bullet holes remained for many weeks afterwards in the shop window of Boots the Chemists and remained for many years afterwards in the walls of what was then Mules's tobacconist shop and men's hairdressing salon in the Square. The latter ones disappeared when the premises were later remodelled by new owners, the Bristol and West Building Society.

My own involvement in the incident was very 'fringe' but nonetheless rather alarming. My father was at that time stationed in Bath with the Admiralty and came home to Launceston at weekends whenever a break from duty permitted. A colleague, whose family was living at Sticklepath, near Okehampton, gave him a lift there and local taxi driver Len Jones (who had garage premises in Guildhall Square) was hired to complete his journey.

On the Sunday evening in question I was going to Sticklepath to meet Father, car rides at that time being a rare luxury. I had walked to town and was to meet Mr Jones outside the Town Hall. I had just arrived at the rendezvous when Mr Jones appeared in his taxi and said would I mind waiting just five minutes as he had a fare whom he was taking to Pennygillam. Not wishing to stand expectantly in such a prominent situation at a time when soldiers were cruising about, I set off to walk towards the Square, intending it to appear that I was hurrying to an appointment, before returning to the Town Hall to meet Mr Jones. As I walked past the Conservative Club I heard some shouting in the Square and decided to cross the road and walk back towards Guildhall Square but just as I got to what was then Messrs Wooldridge's motorcycle repair shop (later Messrs Harris & Hocken's premises and now vacant) all hell broke loose in the direction of the Square. There was shouting and screaming; I clearly remember a woman's piercing scream and another high-pitched shriek which rose above the general din. Then I heard one shot fired. I cowered against the wall of the building, expecting to be engulfed in a running battle spilling down into Western Road. Then, after only a few minutes but what seemed like an eternity, the 'snowdrops' (military police, so nicknamed because they wore white helmets) came roaring along Western Road, jeep after jeep load of them, tyres screeching as they turned into the Square. More shouting, swearing, general hullaballoo - as the action seemed to be confined to the Square I broke cover and scuttled back as fast as I could to the Town Hall, to be met, to my great relief, by Mr Jones in his taxi, which had almost been swept off the road by the careering jeeps. He was shaking almost as much as I was.

The outcome of the incident was that a number of troops faced a court martial at Paignton and rumour had it that the death penalty was imposed on some of the black soldiers involved. This was never known for a fact but the coloured troops could at that time face the ultimate penalty if proved to have committed rape and so it is not unlikely that other serious misdemeanours carried the same penalty. Like so many things that happened concerning the U.S. Army in those extraordinary times no one will ever know for certain. There are still incidents which affected the lives of some of those in Launceston and district which remain to this day and have never been explained. But that is another story.

A few personal ties emerged between the troops stationed locally and local residents and some of the soldiers became quite well-known and popular, with their outgoing personalities and friendly natures, not to mention their generosity in distributing material benefits such as sweets and cigarettes.

Some will never be forgotten. There are probably people in the town today who remember them still; sort of folk heroes who came as if from another planet and enlivened dreary, sad days and drab lives at a time when morale was inevitably low and any diversion was a Godsend. Who remembers 'Lootenant' Johnny Nightingale who had all the girls in a tizzy as he whirled up and down along the B3254 road on his high-powered motorcycle, supervising the coloured troops who built and serviced the ammunition shelters? Johnny was a dashing figure. If he had been a sailor he would have been dubbed the type who has a girl in every port; in this case perhaps it was in every village! He was actually a very nice man and most interesting to talk to, but he was blessed (or cursed) with extremely good looks and an impish smile which together 'slayed' all the girls.

'Lucky' Lee was the Lothario of the coloured troops. 'Lucky' liked Drambuie, a little-recognised drink in Launceston in those days, a fact which he frequently bemoaned, and he could dance divinely. All the local girls almost literally queued up to

THE SECOND MILITARY INVASION

dance with him at local 'hops'. He could make you feel you were Ginger Rogers dancing with Fred Astaire, even if you were convinced you normally had two left feet. He was once described by a more down-to-earth colleague as 'a flirty eyed guy with a slick line of talk', a comment worthy of being included in a book of quotations!

Miss Kitty Parsons, who ran a bakers' shop in Launceston, was besieged almost daily by one of the soldiers who developed a passion for a kind of mincemeat-filled open tart which the baker produced as an occasional luxury item when rations permitted. The boy had never tasted such a thing back in Chicago and he just could not get enough of it. He offered almost literally wads of notes in an effort to persuade the bakers to make him such a tart every day.

During their sojourn in the town the 'darkies' staged a variety show in the Town Hall. It was called "Dixie" and Launceston had never seen anything like it before. Some of the men were professional entertainers and they put on a splendid show with a truly professional touch. For weeks afterwards everybody who saw the show was going around humming a catchy tune, "Chocolate Soldier from the U.S.A.", a popular hit song of the day. Proceeds from the sale of tickets for "Dixie" were given to charity and the whole event was one of the highlights of the year in the town, helping people to forget the tragedy of war just for one evening.

Of course, behind all the innocent novelty and excitement which the foreign 'invasion' caused there was a seamy side. There were the inevitable camp followers and sometimes the court was very busy. The soldiers also owned possessions which were like a dream or fairy tale in a Britain denuded of all luxuries, and such items were understandably tempting to the light fingered. Some residential and commercial properties were requisitioned and sometimes treated in a disgraceful manner: at least one large house was literally uninhabitable after the soldiers left and was eventually demolished.

Cornwall's narrow roads were never intended to be used by huge army trucks and jeeps being driven with all the abandon of a youngster on roller skates. There were a number of accidents involving military vehicles in the area, some fatal. A personal memory is of a large U.S. truck crashing through the parapet of Yeolmbridge bridge and landing on its wheels in the river.

One feature of the American 'invasion', not fully appreciated at the time, was that the whole area was turned into a vast powder keg and a few strategically aimed bombs dropped by the Germans could have resulted in the total devastation of Launceston and all the surrounding countryside. A vast railhead was constructed at Halwill and ammunition was brought into there in huge quantities. It was stored in open-ended Nissen type shelters erected at intervals along main and some secondary roads. The black troops of the Ordnance Battalions were responsible for all the movement and storage of the 'ammo' and hundreds of thousands of tons of explosives must have been stored in the area in comparatively flimsy shelters. Along the B3254 road between Lady Cross and Whitstone and beyond, great gaps suddenly appeared almost overnight in roadside hedges, to be filled with equally stealthy speed by the corrugated iron storage shelters. When the Americans left the area and dismantled the shelters they built up the hedges again but curiously, those portions of hedge which filled the gaps have never, to this day, fully re-established as part of the hedgerow system. It is possible to walk from Langdon Cross to Lady Cross and clearly distinguish each piece of 'new' hedge - no oak seedlings have established themselves, the brambles even seem to stop dead and refuse to encroach, the line of demarcation is almost

National Savings Week parade arriving in the Square, 1944.

THE SECOND MILITARY INVASION

uncanny - and it was nearly fifty years ago that the gaps were filled in. It probably helps if one knows exactly where they were sited and walked past them many, many times without the slightest qualm of fear when they were filled with deadly explosives, but even strangers are surprised and intrigued when the sites are pointed out to them. The shelters were emptied as quickly as they were filled, an almost constant process. The long wooden 'ammo' boxes with rope handles were tossed about like rubber balls. With hindsight it is a miracle a tragedy never occurred.

The U.S. Army was always very co-operative in providing personnel for the quite lavish opening parades for the National Savings Weeks such as 'Salute the Soldier' and 'Wings for Victory'. The comment of the watching public was always the same - 'They don't look as smart as our boys'. Certainly marching skills did seem somewhat lacking in finesse at times.

At the end of August 1943, American troops entertained the children of Launceston to a party. They presented the excited children with chewing gum and candy and, by giving up their own rations for a fortnight, provided something which some of the younger children had never even tasted before - ice cream. It was an occasion that was remembered for years afterwards by those who attended it.

No expense was spared to keep the troops happy. Famous sport and entertainment personalities were brought into the area to perform for the soldiers. Boxer Joe Louis was a huge hit when he visited the big camp for coloured troops at Halwill, and Glenn Miller and his Orchestra performed at Pennygillam, the band members being brought in one or two at a time, presumably so that they should not all be involved at one time in any catastrophe which might occur. The band members were all well-known and highly-paid professional musicians in the U.S.A. and used to luxury living. They were said to hate trailing around the remote places to entertain. They were spoken of with awe by the troops, many of whom were 'small town' boys and would never have had the chance of seeing these big names in the flesh in their own country.

The important military figures did not make themselves scarce either. Generals Eisenhower, Bradley and Greunther all visited Launceston, Eisenhower and Bradley on several occasions. They were treated like royalty and the food and wine flowed during their visits in such variety and quantity as would have seemed almost obscene to the luxury-starved local people, who were expected to get excited about such 'hard tack' dishes as Woolton Pie and carrot cake. Fortunately this was one thing about which the Americans did not boast. If you knew the right people you could sometimes be treated to a bit of left-over exotic cheese or fruit but it was all strictly illegal and those who smuggled it out were always very worried about taking the risk.

The U.S. military authorities that were formerly stationed here presented a Stars and Stripes flag to the Borough of Launceston, and for several years after the end of the war it was flown from the Town Hall on Independence Day, 4th July.

And just a footnote. The residents of South Petherwin used to say that the Americans went out shooting rabbits with machine guns! *Did* they? They never did it in Werrington anyway!

The U.S. Army band plays in Launceston Square at the Wings for Victory National Savings Week, 12th June 1943.

THE SECOND MILITARY INVASION

Launceston men who were in reserved occupations in World War II still served their country in many ways. The Royal Observer Corps Launceston Detachment.
L. to R. Back Row: George Dawe, ? Northey?, Ray Rashley, Tom ?, Stuart Fitze, Stuart Cavey, Gerald Raddall.
Front Row: Eric Hawkins, Alf Perkins, Charlie Bradford, Les Stonelake, Bill Chapman, Arthur Mills.

Launceston Detachment St. John's Ambulance Brigade in World War II. Includes Mr W. G. Mooney, Messrs Bill Chapman, Stuart Martin, Raymond Davey, ? Brendon. Who are the rest?

CHAPTER 9
Trade and Industry

Despite a proliferation of factories in recent years one does not really think of Launceston as an industrial town, yet over the years it has been a centre for several industries, some of them long faded into obscurity as times have changed.

In the 17th and 18th centuries the woollen industry was a large employer of labour in Launceston. The workers in the industry even had their own public house in the town, the Bishop Blaise, a name associated with the cloth industry throughout Europe.

At that time Newport was the mainly industrial area of the town. Town Mills was one of the largest woollen mills, employing a large number of apprentices, all of whom received as their annual 'pay' three pairs of woollen stockings. Hardly great remuneration for a year's hard work. Serge was made at Town Mills for some two hundred years but that operation closed down in the early 1850s.

The little plot of land now known as Newport Rest Garden was once occupied by a serge factory, which was run by a family called Flemming and operated for some two hundred years. It is difficult to imagine today a factory on such small site but it employed a great many people and its products were said to be rated as first class.

Ridgegrove Mills were also at one time woollen mills. At both Ridgegrove and Town Mills there were early Spinning Jennies and in common with workers in the same industry in other parts of the country, the Launceston employees strongly resented these new fangled machines and staged some protests, although the latter were mild in comparison with downright riots in other parts of the country.

The industry gave employment not only to people actually working in the mills: ancillary trades also flourished. Moses Symons was a

The small garden to the right of St. Thomas's Bridge was the site of Flemming's serge factory, and Hender's Tannery is at right.

TRADE AND INDUSTRY

feltmonger, i.e. a dealer in felt, and a highly respected member of the community, but he was the bane of the lives of the Turnpike Trustees because he persistently allowed rubbish (presumably connected with his trade) to spill on to the turnpike road, impeding traffic.

Another busy mill stood on the site of what is now Greenaways Garage. It was Court Leet Mill and had a 'branch' in St. Stephens Hill, although just where is not known. Incidentally, a Court Leet was a Court of Record held once a year by the Steward of a Hundred, Lordship or Manor.

In the late 18th and early 19th centuries Launceston was the centre of a thriving straw-hat making industry; it was, in fact, said to have rivalled at one time the famous straw-hat town of Luton. It employed mostly women and a large army of 'outworkers' who did the work in their own homes. A spin-off from this was milliners, of whom there were a number residing in the town at that time, making and trimming hats not only for the local well-to-do ladies but also for customers far afield. A Miss Grylls, "milliner of distinction", advertised regularly in "The Sherborne Mercury" and boasted "satisfaction to a large clientele".

A rather messier and certainly more odoriferous trade which centred on Newport was tanning. At least three tanneries are known to have existed in close proximity to the river Kensey, the best known of which was Henders, which did not cease trading until 1963. It produced superb hides and in 1920 won a prestigious award for hides tanned without the use of chemicals. The art of preparing the tan was the closely guarded secret of the head tanner, who used personally to collect oak bark and sumach leaves in nearby woods. The famous Hender's tannery building with its louvred upper façade, the 'walls' of the drying floors, which enabled air to circulate around the hides laid out to dry, was a landmark at Newport until the 1980s when it was shamelessly demolished and another valuable part of Launceston's history disappeared for ever. There were two more such buildings almost adjoining St. Thomas's Church and facing the Kensey, but these were demolished in comparatively recent times to make way for the building of St. Thomas Church Hall. *Now*, when it is too late, planning is more stringent and bodies such as the Department of the Environment and English Heritage ensure that what is our heritage is protected.

Were our ancestors obsessed with time? It would seem so, because between the mid 18th century and the late 19th century there were no fewer than twenty five watch and clockmakers in Launceston, including George Routleigh (1745-1802) who is buried in Lydford churchyard, Devon, with a famous epitaph on his table tomb. John Box, who had premises in Westgate Street and then in Broad Street, is remembered to this day as his longcase (grandfather) clocks are highly prized and anyone owning a John Box grandfather clock has a valuable antique on their hands. In the early 18th century clockmaker and gunsmith Digory Pendray

In this wintry scene the building next to St. Thomas Church was originally a tannery building. Note the louvred upper floor.

TRADE AND INDUSTRY

Hender's Tannery. Again, note the louvred front on the upper floor. This was where skins were laid out to dry: the louvred front allowed air to circulate. This tannery was demolished in 1980.

received £2.00 a year for "keeping the town clocks". Launceston was, indeed, at one time the watch and clockmaking 'capital' of the south west.

Disused quarries abound in the neighbourhood: few farms do not have the remains of old quarrying scars on their land. Quarrying is one of the oldest industries in which man busied himself; stone was always there and it had a myriad of uses. Around the Launceston area quarries varied from the small excavation from which a farmer dug stone for field boundary walls to larger 'holes' which provided stone for building and for road maintenance in later years, to the really big undertakings which expanded very considerably in the 19th century. Yeolmbridge Quarry came into the latter category: owned by the Milnes family, who lived in a large house at Yeolmbridge, it was very deep and large in extent, it employed a great many men and it was an industrial complex of some magnitude for those days. Its slate was said to be superior even to the famous Delabole slate, being more impervious to heat.

Barricadoes Quarry, at the top of Barricadoes Hill, also produced slate which was particularly in demand for gravestones. The late Mr Northey, stonemason at Grant's Monumental Works at the end of Winsor Cottages at Newport, was a regular customer there and as late as the years right up to the outbreak of World War II he could often be seen setting off with his wheelbarrow to select a piece of slate for a gravestone, later returning with it loaded in the barrow and having considerable difficulty in controlling the unwieldy load on the steepish slope of Roydon Road before crossing the Dutson road and right into his yard. It was fascinating to stand there and watch him carving an inscription, painstakingly chipping away at each letter and making a beautiful job of it. No machine-made and implanted lettering in those days.

Mention has already been made in another chapter of the mining boom as it affected the Launceston area. Almost all traces have vanished now. In Lawrence House Museum there are documents relating to the finances of the St. Stephens Manganese Co. which started in 1875 but no one even knows now just where the mining operations took place; they were said to have been in a field on the west side of Barricadoes plantation but there are no clues left.

In 1944 ploughing in a pasture near Truscott turned up quantities of pyrolusite with quartz and this was immediately used by the farmer for building up hedges. In Cannapark Wood the traces of old dumps are still faintly visible. The now popular residential village of Langore was originally a mining village: manganese was worked there and a cart track known as Church Lane was believed to be a short cut to the mines at Truscott. A well close to an adit on Langore Green was the village's water supply before the mains services were installed. On Atway Farm there is still an enclosure known as Mine Field where faint traces of an open shaft still exist.

Perhaps the most bizarre story of mining operations in the Launceston area is that in 1843 an artesian well was being sunk in Broad Street when a large copper lode of superior quality was uncovered. The town council immediately refused a frantic application for permission for mining to be allowed - on the grounds that mining beneath

TRADE AND INDUSTRY

the town would deprive inhabitants of water by causing all the wells to run dry. So the lode is still there and is reputed to be one of the richest in Cornwall, although, of course, time may have caused its productivity value to be magnified!

Many people will remember when brick making was an industry which employed quite a lot of men in the town. The brickworks at Dutson with its tall chimney and in the latter years before its final disappearance, the finest clumps of primroses to be seen anywhere, which adorned the lane leading into it. The brickworks came to service the Bude Canal when it was planned to take the canal from Druxton Wharf to Ridgegrove Mill and beyond. That scheme never materialised but long after the canal closed down bricks were still being made at Dutson.

We have left till the last one of the important industries in the town that was still carried on into modern times and one of its most skilful exponents was still practising it right up to the time of his death in 1991. That most useful and most skilful of all crafts was ropemaking. Ropemaking was a very important industry to a farming community and Launceston still has a memorial to it in the footpath known today as The Walk. This thoroughfare was at one time part of the old town wall; later it became used as a promenade by the townspeople and some attractive villas were built along its length, overlooking spectacular views along the Kensey valley to Dartmoor and beyond. In the 18th and 19th centuries the long, straight pathway was put to good use as a ropewalk, being ideal for the purpose, and thus it got its modern name.

A few years ago I had the pleasure and privilege of interviewing Mr Bill Maunder, a very skilled ropemaker from an old Launceston family of such craftsmen, and was able to see finished examples of

The late Mr Bill Maunder was a master craftsman ropemaker. He is shown with a tool at an exhibition which he staged at Launceston Museum.

his work, as well as photographing him actually using, with his son, the antique equipment for making ropes which he had set up on an upper floor of his firm's extensive modern premises on the outskirts of the town.

The firm of Maunder was started in 1850 by Joseph ('Happy Joe') Maunder who learnt the trade from Valentine Poad in a ropewalk which was at one time located on the corner of Exeter Street, Launceston, where the Christian Bookshop now stands, and the Poad family also ran a bakery in Exeter Street. Up until 1860 the rope was actually made right across the road, one end being started in Mr Poad's passageway and attached to the primitive apparatus set up on the other side of the street. Presumably there was not much traffic to impede this process in those days!

'Happy Joe' started his business in 1890, working hard to build it up by hawking ropes around the local markets. He used to make his ropes in the back garden of his home in Race Hill, starting at 4am to comb the hemp and then working on until dark to get his stock ready to carry to market. By 1900 he had progressed to a stall selling ropes in Launceston market and after his son Richard joined him in the business they opened a shop in Race Hill. In the ropewalk behind the shop Mr Bill Maunder learned the craft, taught by his grandfather and starting by making rabbit nets. He soon became very skilled and used to make halters, cow ties, cart reins, bull ropes, pig nets, burden rope, plough reins, bell ropes, whipcord, rabbit nets and head halters. He was one of the last people in the South West able to repair a bell rope at both ends, a highly skilled operation. Mr Maunder recalled that cow ties cost 3d each and plough reins 2/-. In 1936 a new bell rope cost £5, new bottom end £1.10.0 and a new top end £2. In the very early days prices were even lower because there was keen competition between the firms of Maunder and Poad.

Now the once flourishing trade of ropemaking in Launceston has disappeared for ever. Mr Bill Maunder's son John can also make rope, taught by his father and grandfather, but with a large business supplying hardware, farmers' supplies etc. to run from premises at Pennygillam he no longer has time to practise the craft. The last ropewalk in Launceston was built by Mr Joe Maunder behind his home at Laurel Cottage, Race Hill, and before moving to Pennygillam the firm had expanded to take in the former C. H. Gillbard's wool store in Race Hill, the building which now houses an antiquarian bookshop. Knowing this book was in preparation, Mr Bill Maunder was pleased to provide this information and to give permission for it to be published. Sadly he did not live to see it in print, but would be pleased to know that it has been preserved for posterity.

Mr Bill Maunder making rope with his original equipment.

TRADE AND INDUSTRY

One of the first motorised vehicles in Launceston stands outside Prockter's shop in Southgate Street. It is believed to have belonged to Dr Budd.

One of the first steam lorries in Launceston.

Mr Tom Jenkins drove one of the early petrol-driven lorries in Launceston.

TRADE AND INDUSTRY

When Mr Davey founded the long-established butchery business of W. W. Davey (now Messrs Philip Warren & Son) in Launceston he started with a horse-drawn delivery cart in his home parish of St. Giles in the Heath.

Mr and Mrs W. Davey in later life, when their sons had taken over the business.

Messrs W. & W. Davey's shop at 1 Westgate Street prior to being acquired by Mr W. Davey.

TRADE AND INDUSTRY

Mr Stanley Davey and Miss Winnie Davey (later Mrs Hooper) flank friend Mr Vosper of Callington outside their father's shop in the late 1930s.

Times have changed and now Mr Henry Symons delivers to customers of Philip Warren & Son with a modern van. Mr Symons was still employed by Messrs W. & W. Davey when this picture was taken.

TRADE AND INDUSTRY

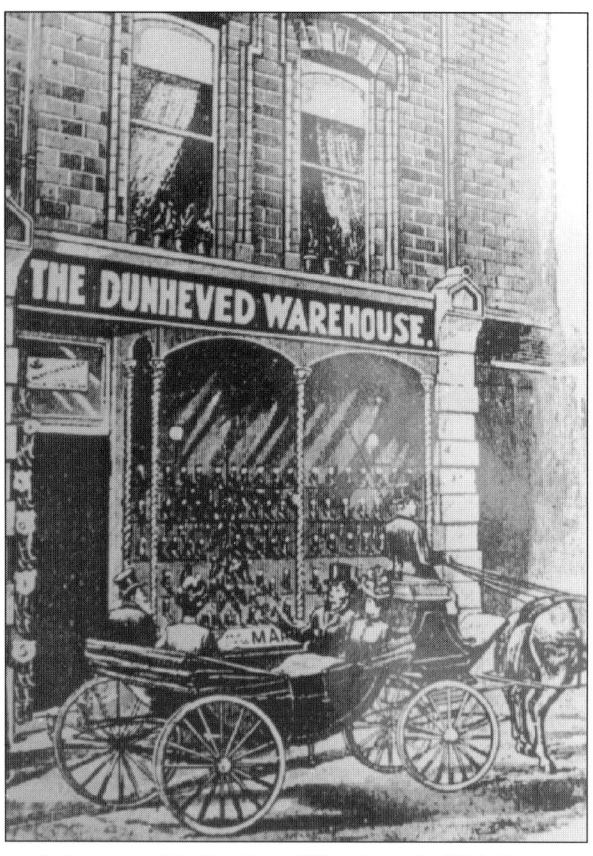

A drawing of the Dunheved Warehouse in High Street, which sold footwear in Victorian times.

Mr Horace Robbins's Northgate Garage Cycle Works in Northgate Street was patronised by all the "young bloods" of the town in the early 1930s, before motor cycles took over.

Many Launcestonians will remember going up the wooden stairs (with the "Ring the Daisy Bell" instruction at the bottom) to the Launceston Printing Co. premises in Race Hill, and seeing type being set up by hand. The letters were plucked at lightning speed from the compartmented wooden type trays.

CHAPTER 10
Launceston Miscellany

LOOK UPWARDS!

If we always keep our eyes to the ground we miss an awful lot! That is particularly true of a search for interesting features in a town. If we cast our eyes upwards occasionally we shall see and learn quite a lot about that town and its history and Launceston is no exception.

Many of us scuttle up and down Blindhole, that narrow lane between the King's Arms hostelry and Southgate which is a short cut to the health centre, but few are aware of an interesting feature high up on the wall of the King's Arms. It is a little bellcote contraption protruding from the wall; it is minus its bell now but it once served a very useful purpose. As explained in another chapter, Blindhole was once a busy and crowded thoroughfare and stables figured prominently among the many buildings which lined it. On market days farmers and landowners 'parked' their horses and conveyances there and after they had done their business they repaired to the King's Arms for lunch and a convivial drink with friends. Most were regular customers, well-known to the landlord, and to most of them that bell was important. Each regular customer was allocated a 'code' for the ringing of the bell. For instance, Mr A. would have two sharp tolls of the bells, Mr B. might have three tolls, Mr C. might have two tolls then a pause, then another toll and so on. When the gentlemen were ready to leave, after having dined and supped well, they informed the landlord and he then tolled the bell according to their personal code. This was the signal for the ostler (perhaps the customer's personal servant, perhaps the inn's man) to take to the front entrance the horse, pony or whatever equipage had been 'parked' in the Blindhole stables, ready for the customer to ride or drive away. A little bit of Launceston history which died when the age of the motor car dawned.

Look upward at the cistern heads on the downpipes of Castle Hill House. They bear the arms of Jago quartered Trelawny. Castle Hill House is believed to have been built by a member of the Jago family about 1730. The Jagos lived in it until about 1814 and represented the Pelynt branch of the Trelawny family. In Baring-Gould's book "Old Country Life" the house was the subject of an engraving, as were Dockacre House, Southgate, the late Dr Andrews's house (now Copeland House) and the old London Inn.

The Jago/Trelawny coat of arms on a down pipe of Castle Hill House.

75

Look upward above the main entrance to the White Hart Hotel in the Square and directly beneath a window on the top floor will be seen a sculpted stone head. Mr Arthur Venning was able to confirm that it depicts Thomas Chandler Haliburton, Mr Justice Haliburton Q.C., a Canadian who came to England on his retirement and was a Launceston M.P. who was nominated for the post by the last Duke of Northumberland to own Werrington Park. Incidentally, during the Assizes the Sheriff and his troop always lodged at the White Hart.

Look upwards, too, at Newport, when emerging from the industrial estate (once the road into the Great Western Railway station). Facing that road are two houses in St. Thomas Road which are decorated high up with the terracotta plaques and mouldings which were so fashionable in Victorian times. With classical designs of acanthus leaves, Tudor roses etc. they were produced at the Tamar Firebrick Works at Cox Park, near Gunnislake, and are probably unique now. When the Firebrick Works closed down hundreds of these plaques and mouldings were left lying around, discarded and for anyone to pick up. Now the site is a caravan park and a housing estate and all traces of the terracotta ware have long gone.

Look upwards at the identical moulded female heads on the façade of a large house in Church Stile, opposite St. Mary's Church Path. Contrary to popular belief they do not have any special significance. They were merely added as ornamentation when this fine Georgian town house, which was originally of two storeys, had an extra storey added in about 1900. They are an attractive feature decorating the window head keystones. Incidentally, it can easily be seen today where the extra storey was built on.

Stand back a moment and look above your head as you prepare to go through the small arched entrance to the Health Centre. It will be seen that the granite lintel has carved on it 'N B BEGAN 1611'. This was the entrance door lintel to a garden known in the 17th century as Polholme Garden or le Polme Garden, suggested by some historians as presumably being the pomme (apple) garden or orchard. Another theory is that it meant palm garden, which sounds more likely. There was also, it is believed, a manor house in these grounds and this door lintel was probably the entrance to that building rather than the garden itself. N. B. were the initials of the house owner, Nicholas Baker, who was mayor in 1610-1611. The Polholme Garden (or Polhomme, as it is sometimes written) formed a portion of the present churchyard and included the area on which the health office (formerly St. Mary's Vicarage) now stands. It extended as far as the old town wall, which can be traced opposite Dockacre House and behind new dwellings up Angel Hill to the South Gate.

MATTERS MILITARY

There are few places in Launceston more pleasant for stopping and taking a short rest on a summer's day than the open tarmacked space below St. Mary's Church Path known as the Militiamen's Parade Ground. This charming spot, with ancient slate steps at one end, leading down to Dockacre Road, is an ideal vantage point for examining the invulnerability of Launceston from the east in ancient times, for it is from here that it can best be observed how steep was the approach to the town from that direction. There are also wonderful views across the Kensey valley to Dartmoor and beyond, with Brentor clearly visible in one direction and the tors behind Okehampton in the other. Seats thoughtfully placed beneath the lime trees offer a delightful invitation to relax and enjoy the view.

But the open space behind was not always so peaceful. When it was feared that Napoleon would invade England the town of Launceston, in common with many other towns, raised its army of Fencibles, The Launceston & Newport Volunteers, (somewhat equivalent to the Territorial Army today) and this was their parade ground. Many were the local lads who did their 'square bashing' on that ground. A few years ago there was an irresponsible suggestion that this historic site in the town should be turned into a car park. Heaven forbid such a thing ever happening to it!

For what may have been thought of as a sleepy country town, far from the hub of military activity, Launceston had quite a military past.

In 1794 Mr Edward Archer of Trelaske, Sheriff of Cornwall, headed fifty men, a sergeant, a corporal, a drummer and a fifer as The Volunteers of Lewannick, South Petherwin, North Hill and Lezant marched into town and in Broad Street launched a recruiting drive "with the Royal Standard hoisted on a hogshead of strong ale, a trumpet calling attention to the cause and the quartermaster parading the street on his charger", but sadly "this did not seem to attract many recruits" says a contemporary report.

The Launceston Volunteers were at one time quite a force with which to reckon. An interesting old document which still exists relates to a Cornish Volunteer Commission in 1808 addressed by "Richard, Earl of Mount Edgcumbe, Viscount

TRADE AND INDUSTRY

Messrs Arthur Wills, Eddie Dart (Hon. Curator) and Breyhan (Tchic) Gilyead on the occasion of the presentation of a cheque to cover the cost of a showcase for the Fencible's uniform (Newport Volunteers) seen in the background.

Valletort, Baron Edgcumbe of Mount Edgcumbe in the County of Devon, Lord Lieutenant of the County of Cornwall, to David Thompson, Gentleman". It goes on to appoint Mr Thompson "to be an Ensign in the Corps of Launceston and Newport Volunteer Infantry, but not to take Rank in the Army, except during the time of the said Corps being called into actual Service". Which proves that the Launceston & Newport Volunteers were prepared to go into battle wherever they were needed. Incidentally, that appointment was dated 6th January 1808 and on 9th August of the same year Ensign Thompson was promoted by Lord Mount Edgcumbe to the rank of Lieutenant in the Corps of Launceston and Newport Volunteers.

In his booklet "Lawrence House, Launceston" (obtainable from the Museum) the late Mr H. Spencer Toy speaks of Humphry Lawrence the second raising a company of the Essex Light Dragoons in Launceston in 1796 and between that date and 1803 when the regiment was disbanded in Inniskilling, Ireland, it was stationed in various places around England as well as in Scotland. Mr Toy records that the members were called Fencibles to distinguish them from Regulars. A miniature of Capt. Humphry Lawrence in the uniform of his regiment is among the treasures to be seen in the Museum today.

CORONATION EXPENSES, 17th CENTURY STYLE

King Charles II died at noon on Friday, 6th February 1685 but the news did not reach Launceston until the following Thursday. Immediately there was feverish activity to inform the populace and on 12th February the sum of £3.11.8 was disbursed from the borough funds as "Expenses when the King was proclaimed". On 23rd April there was another recorded payment - "Exp.: Attend the Coronation £2.8.6".

What is interesting from the same document in the town archives is a "List of necessary Expenses of the Mayoral yr." These include:-

Pd. ye Gunsmith's Bill 13/6
fower Red Coats for ye Soldiers	£4.16.0
Mnths pay to fower Soldiers for ye Town Arme	£5.12.0
Messenger that came from Sir Hugh Piper with message about Callington business	2/-
Messenger sent to Plymouth to Sir Hugh Piper to aquaint him of My Lord of Bath's coming here	4/-
for beere for ye Ringers had at Squire's when My Lord of Bath came first to town	2/-
For beere and bisketts at ye speech house when ye Address was signed	1/8
For a seame of wood on ye newes of ye taking Monmouth	1/2
Ye Musick by consent of ye Aldermen	5/-
seame of wood ye day of rejoicing on ye newes of ye King's recovery	1/2
Monmouth taccan the ringers	2/6
wood for a bunfire	1/2

The somewhat cryptic entry of 'Monmouth taccan' referred to Monmouth being captured (taken) and the bells being rung in the town in celebration of that event.

Incidentally, the Earl of Bath was son of Sir Bevil Grenville.

Bygone Launceston
A selection of photographs of scenes not specifically referred to in the text

DAYS OF STEAM

Launceston Railway Stations seen from Zig Zag. The photograph is believed to date from the late 1890s.

Egloskerry was once a busy station on the Southern Railway line to Padstow.

DAYS OF STEAM

The much loved Atlantic Coast Express - Waterloo to Padstow - at Launceston Southern Railway Station in the early 1960s.

Queen Elizabeth II arrives at Launceston Station.

TRANSPORT

The Royal Mail delivery cart in Smith's Castle Hotel stables in 1912. The horse and cart were both kept at this venue. The driver is Mr Parish.

Miss Gurney prepares to take her puppy for a ride in her donkey shay.

TRANSPORT

Miss Mabel Maddever was a familiar figure around Launceston in her Austin 7 car. Miss Maddever, a retired teacher, sold the car nearly 40 years ago and it was later restored by its present owners, Mr and Mrs Gill of Hayle, seen here with Miss Maddever and car in 1987.

Egloskerry had three mobile postmen on bicycles, one postman on foot, one on horseback, and a cart for parcel post in about 1910. Among the postmen shown here are Messrs Symons senior and junior, Mr Jenkins, Mr Frayn on the horse and Mr Grylls the sub-postmaster in the centre.

"LANSON" LOOKED LIKE THIS

Two views of Newport and St. Stephens, showing how the area gradually got built up over the years. When the first photograph was taken Roydon Road was still known as Zulu Road.

"LANSON" LOOKED LIKE THIS

Egloskerry used to have a public house and when it lost that it gained a telephone kiosk. The Simcoe Arms had as its inn sign the coat of arms of the Simcoe family, one-time squires who lived at Penheale, now the home of the Colvilles. One member of the Simcoe family was Vicar of Egloskerry for many years.

"LANSON" LOOKED LIKE THIS

Who remembers Castle Green like this?

"Paradise" was a popular spot for sitting to sun oneself in the Castle grounds.

When Mr R. Tolman and his predecessors tended the Castle grounds they looked like this.

"LANSON" LOOKED LIKE THIS

The Castle and the Castle Green were once well guarded.

Dunheved Road before the car age.

THE ORIGIN OF DUNHEVED ROAD.

LINKED WITH LAUNCESTON'S 1869 MAYOR.

How Dunheved Road came into being is told in the "East Cornwall Times" for November 13, 1869, in an editorial comment on the election as Mayor of Launceston for that year of Mr. John Dingley.

The newspaper stated: "There is one matter in which our new Mayor has displayed his public spirit in a marked degree, and it will be recognised by all without distinction of either politics or religion.

"It is well-known that many visitors whom the railway has attracted to Launceston have been so impressed with its peculiarly healthy situation, the purity of the air circulating amid its hills and valleys, the magnificent stretch of scenery to be witnessed from the town and its approaches, and the beautiful variety of its promenades, that they have expressed a wish to take up their abode in such an eminently pleasant locality.

"The difficulty has been that we have no suitable houses to offer; hence population has remained stationary, enterprise has been discouraged, and trade has not progressed to that extent which may have been desired.

"With a veiw to opening up building sites and thus leading the way for renewed activity, Mr. Dingley has formed one of a party of gentlemen who, at their own expense, have had a new road cut from a point near the Western Subscription Rooms to Badash Cross.

"Those who have gone over that line of route will recognise at a glance the beautiful character of the drive into the town, and the particularly pleasant nature of the sites presented for the operations of the builder.

"On a gentle slope, and protected from the bleak winds which at times sweep down from the north and east, the dwellers in the projected new houses will be favoured with a view which a resident in the suburbs of many a large town would envy. There they will have village and hamlet, and parish church, vale, hillside and streamlet, in one of the prettiest pictures which nature has painted in the West of England."

Article courtesy "Cornish & Devon Post".

"LANSON" LOOKED LIKE THIS

Dunheved College long before expansion.

An early postcard of Dockacre House, one of the oldest houses in the town.

"LANSON" LOOKED LIKE THIS

Polson Bridge was quite a feat of engineering when it was constructed.

The old chain bridge has long gone. This photograph was taken prior to World War II.

"LANSON" LOOKED LIKE THIS

Various attempts have been made over the years to tidy up the ruins of the Augustinian Priory.

WHEN PEOPLE GET TOGETHER

The children of Launceston School look very demure when photographed it is believed about 1910.

Egloskerry School used to be held in the Church Hall at the turn of the century.

WHEN PEOPLE GET TOGETHER

The Sloman Family Orchestra from Warbstow was very well known and much in demand to play at both family and public functions in the area. The soldier and outsize policeman on the right of the top photograph were orchestra members absent on the day, so their pictures have been pasted in.

WHEN PEOPLE GET TOGETHER

The first Boxing Day meet in The Square after World War I.

Harvest Festival was a very important occasion at Middlewood Methodist Chapel, North Hill, prior to World War II.

WHEN PEOPLE GET TOGETHER

Members of Launceston Young Farmers' Club in the 1950s proudly display trophies won by the Club.

A famous snooker player (second from left in this picture) came to Launceston Conservative Club in the 1950s to give a demonstration, but nobody seem to be able to remember who he was! The others shown (L. to R.) are: Mr McCarthy, Wyndham Hender, Ted Harry, John Bale, Bert Tremain (captain), Les Stonelake and Bill Chapman.

WHEN PEOPLE GET TOGETHER

All the family joined in croust time at harvest.

CONCLUSION

In common with all towns, Launceston is forever changing; the march of progress cannot be halted and one cannot help but wonder what those who used the drovers' roads would think of today's bypass, or what the town would be like today if, like Llantrisant, it was chosen for the site of the Royal Mint, following in the wake of the mint at St. Stephens.

    Probably the greatest changes have occurred in the past two decades and who knows what the next two will bring? But the past is important too and gradually, piece by piece, the whole history of Launceston is being assembled. It is hoped that between the covers of this book a little more has been revealed and that as time unfolds, so yet more facets of our town's history will come to light. It has much to offer and much still to tell us.

OTHER BOOKS FROM LANDFALL PUBLICATIONS

LANDFALL WALKS BOOKS

by Bob Acton, "....who leads the field for walking books in Cornwall both in output and content."
(Des Hannigan, writing in the "St Ives Times & Echo", June 1993)

All the books provide detailed directions, sketch maps, information about places and other features of interest, and practical suggestions regarding parking, public transport, refreshments, etc. All are liberally illustrated with drawings, and many also contain numerous photographs.

No. 1 **A VIEW FROM CARN MARTH,** Seven Walks amid Cornwall's Industrial Past (1989) £2.50 (Now out of print. See No. 9.)
No. 2 **A VIEW FROM ST AGNES BEACON,** Eight Walks amid Cornwall's Industrial Past (1989) £2.75
No. 3 **AROUND THE FAL,** Circular Walks (1989, reprinted 1991) £2.95 "The book has been so well written and contains so much varied information that it is enjoyable just to pick up and read." (Review in the "West Briton")
No. 4 **AROUND THE HELFORD,** Circular Walks (1989, reprinted 1990) £2.95
No. 5 **AROUND NEWQUAY,** Circular Walks from Bedruthan to Holywell (1990, revised and enlarged 1993) £3.30
No. 6 **A VIEW FROM CARN BREA,** Circular Walks around Redruth, Camborne and Portreath (1990) £2.95
No. 7 **AROUND THE RIVER FOWEY,** Circular Walks (1990, revised and enlarged 1992) £3.30
No. 8 **AROUND PADSTOW,** Circular Walks from Porthcothan to Wadebridge and Bodmin (1991) £3.30
No. 9 **A SECOND VIEW FROM CARN MARTH** Fourteen Round walks near Truro, Falmouth and Redruth (1991) Colour photographs. £4.95
No.10 **AROUND ST AUSTELL,** Circular Walks from Pentewan to Par (1992) Colour photographs. £3.30
No.11 **AROUND MEVAGISSEY,** Circular Walks from Portscatho to Pentewan (1992) Colour photographs. £3.30
No.12 **A VIEW FROM TRENCROM,** Round Walks near Hayle, St Ives and Penzance (1993) £3.30 "A must for the student of the past industry of West Cornwall - whether a local or a summer visitor." (Newsletter of the Trevithick Society)
No.13 **A VIEW FROM CARN GALVER,** Mining Trails in the Far South West (1993) Colour photographs. £4.95 (Covers the area from St Just to St Ives and Madron, and was described in the Bulletin of the Bristol Industrial Archaeological Society as "the best guide for walkers in any area of industrial archaeological interest that I have yet seen.")

OTHER LANDFALL BOOKS

THE LANDFALL BOOK OF TRURO by Bob Acton (1990) £1.25 (City maps plus five walks in and around Truro)

THE LANDFALL BOOK OF THE POLDICE VALLEY by Bob Acton (1990) £3.99 This book looks in some detail at the history of a district, just south of St Day, which for several decades was the world's main source of copper. Short, medium and longer walks and rides are described. "... packed with information ... an excellent companion to those who wish to explore the district on their own." (Newsletter of the Northern Mines Research Society)

ST IVES HERITAGE, Recollections and Records of St Ives, Carbis Bay and Lelant, by Lena and Donald Bray (First published in 1981 by Dyllansow Truran; revised edition with many new photographs, Landfall Publications 1992) £5.99 "Lena and Donald's wonderful book should find an essential place on the bookshelves of anyone who seeks to remember and understand the real heritage of St Ives Bay." (Des Hannigan)

NEWQUAY'S PICTORIAL PAST A book of old photographs originally published by the Newquay Old Cornwall Society in 1983, and re-issued ten years later in a revised version by Landfall. £3.00

LIFE BY THE FAL, Years of Change at Point and Penpol, by Viv Acton (1993) Colour photographs. £4.95 A detailed study of a small waterside community near Devoran that was caught up in Cornwall's Industrial Revolution. "A first class piece of writing and research." (Peter Gilson)

PRIMROSE TIME, A Cornish Childhood Remembered, by Mary Baker (1993) £3.99 Mary, now in her eighties, remembers with extraordinary vividness her earliest experiences in life. The setting is Lelant, Hayle and St Ives, but the true subject is childhood, and here it is presented as it were from the inside, without sentimentality but with a delicious sense of humour.

In case of difficulty in obtaining any of the above books, contact:
LANDFALL PUBLICATIONS, Landfall, Penpol, Devoran, Truro, Cornwall TR3 6NW (0872-862581)

Please add 20% to the above prices to cover the costs of postage and packing,
up to a maximum of £5.00.